Moments With Melinda

Collection of stories, songs, and poems

By Melinda Sutherland

Copyright and Disclaimer

Biblical References are from the NLT (New Living Translation)

Cover Photography by
Connie Filip, Ocala, Florida

Published by
SWL Media and Learning Center
Ocala, Florida 34481 www.SWLMedia.com

ISBN: 9798552404490

Acknowledgments

First and foremost to God, who gave me the blessing of family and friends who have been there for me. My husband John, who always supported my adventures, be it listening in the audience or lugging my equipment. My children Destini, Damon, and Dustin and their respective spouses, Ray, Lena, and Maki. My beautiful grandchildren Belinda, Matthew, James, Reagan, Tatum, Nikita, Lukas.

Cover and jacket picture by Connie Filip, a neighbor, friend, and amazing photographer.

Dedication

Ever since I was a young girl, at family gatherings, the story of my Cousin Myrna biting me on the behind was told. Little did I know that was just the start of her pushing me along - at least I like to look at it as she pushed me along and not out of her way. Over the years, she has been a sounding board for my stories, songs, and poems. She read, listened, critiqued, and proofread them. It is with great pride I dedicate this book to my Cousin, Myrna.

Table *of Contents*

Section One - Chapters to Grow On

This section consists of people and places in my life when I was a child. Little did I know the significance these experiences would have on me as I was growing up until the storyteller in me awakened.

A Real Girl

Chapter One - 4-H Cooking Project

I was the exception!

All women on my mother's side refers to themselves as being "a real girl." That means they like to cook, or should I say they love to cook. Family gatherings meant sitting around, swapping recipes, hour after hour after hour. I was dragged to these "hen cacklings" reluctantly. Mother thought that if I listened long enough, the spirit would move me to want to run into the kitchen, whip up a cake, and become a real girl.

Mother soon realized these hen gatherings weren't working. She came up with another plan. My sister Debbie and I would join a 4-H club to learn how to cook. Now, I had no objection to Debbie's doing this because she was already a real girl. Not only could she cook, she did dreadful things like wearing fingernail polish, putting ribbons in her hair, and playing with dolls. I had more important things to do. I had to organize the neighborhood baseball game and help build a treehouse.

My cooking project was to make a cake from scratch, by myself, to enter in the Kankakee County fair. I had to do this on Saturday when mother took her weekly trip into town. Her shopping trips didn't end until she heard, "Attention shoppers, our store will be closing in fifteen minutes, please bring all final purchases to the front registers."

Saturday came, and I waited for my mother to leave. I got out my 4-H cooking book with the recipe in it to do a practice run. I gathered up all the ingredients and started to read the directions, only to discover they were in a foreign language. I had no idea that a teesp, or tasp, or ozzzes of things were a teaspoon, tablespoon, or ounces of things. I had only heard of a smidgen of this, a handful of this, a dash of that, and a pinch of this from all the "hen cackling" get-togethers. I thought, "Great, now I'm doomed. I will never be a real girl." I then spied the measuring cup I used to put sugar in the Kool-Aid. I figured if it was good enough for my Kool-Aid, it was good enough for this dumb old cake. I put in a cup of sugar, a cup of salt, a cup of baking powder, a cup of baking soda, a cup of eggs, a cup of flour, and a cup of cocoa. It called for vanilla, but I didn't see any, so I put in a cup of vinegar. Mother used vinegar in other recipes, and since they both started with a V, I thought it to be a good idea.

I started mixing the cake when suddenly the bowl turned into a Tupperware volcano spitting out a river of brown lava. Dad was out in the garage, working on our car. I hollered, "Dad help me! My

5

cake is alive!" He got a bigger bowl, and it overflowed. He looked at me and said, "Mem, I reckon we'd better throw it away." He carried the bowl filled with batter to the garbage can out in the utility room. We started to leave, and we heard "blump, blump, blump." My cake was coming out of the garbage can. Dad said, "Mem, I reckon we'd better take it out to the burn barrel." We both picked up the garbage can and ran outside to the burn barrel. We lit the match before the cake started to grow anymore.

We turned to leave when we heard, "blump, blump, blump." My cake was slowly rising out of the burn barrel! Dad hollered at me to get the shovels. For what seemed like an eternity, we shoveled my never-ending cake back into the burn barrel. Finally, we won over the glob. Exhausted, we walked back to the house. We froze in our tracks when we saw a car in the driveway. Mother arrived home from shopping much earlier than expected. Seeing her kitchen, which is her sanctuary, she let out this high pitched, blood-curdling scream. It made the hair stand up on the back of our necks. Dogs were howling and running to our house.

I was banned from the kitchen until I was 105.

Chapter Two - Cooking with Mamo

The following week our family set out for our yearly vacation to Tennessee. Our first stop was Columbia to see Mamo, our city grandma. We usually got there about 2:00 in the morning. Mamo always wanted to fix us something to eat. Mother insisted we didn't need anything, but it was Mamo's house, and Mamo won. There I am at 2:00 in the morning eating my very own chocolate moon pie and drinking my very own bottle of Coca-Cola when Mamo leans over to me and says, "Heard ya had a little trouble cookin'." Of course, that was putting it quite mildly. "How'd ya like to sleep with me tonight, and then in the morning you can help me make my cinnamon bread?" Mamo was well known for her cinnamon bread, and now I was going to get to help her. I yelled "Yes!" I finished off my chocolate moon pie and Coca-Cola. Then I got ready for bed.

I loved Mamo's bedroom. When you came out of the kitchen door, on the wall to the left was her oak four-post feather bed. Next to the bed was a window that went from the floor to the ceiling, and next to the window was her chest of drawers that matched her bed. Coming around to the next wall was Mamo's closet. Next to her closet was a fireplace, with a white mantle that held her clock and family pictures. Two rocking chairs were placed at each end of the mantle. Next to the fireplace was a door that led to the parlor, where guests were entertained. In the connecting wall there was a door that led to the flushing toilet in the hallway. Mamo's matching vanity and bench next to the door. In the middle of the vanity was a big round mirror with drawers on each side that held her hair supplies and make-up.

It was a big excitement when Mamo installed a flushing toilet. Mamo was very thrifty about her flushing toilet, as it cost money to use. Since you couldn't flush the Sears Roebuck catalog down the commode, toilet paper was rationed. And flushing cost money, so you were only allowed so many flushes a day. I thought since we no longer had to go to the outhouse, we could at least use the flushing toilet for the night, but as I was getting into bed, Mamo went to the bathroom and got "the pot." It was a white ceramic pail of about twelve inches high, with a white lid that had a red ring around the edge. The lid had a wooden handle for easier lifting. This would be our facilities for the night.

She placed it between the rockers and then locked all three doors, letting no one in and no one out. Mamo went over to the chest of drawers, opened the top drawer, and pulled out her gun. She told me in detail how people break into old widow women's houses and rob them. She said they weren't comin' into her house. She was ready for 'em. She polished her gun with the hem of her nightgown before carefully placing it back in the top drawer. There was always a gleam in Mamo's eyes when she was talking about her gun.

She said it was time for us to go to bed, and I said, "Yes, Ma'am." Mamo laid down at the foot of the bed. She said it was cooler sleeping there cause the breeze came through the window. I think Mamo was waiting for the robbers. I laid at the head, planning my escape should they come.

About an hour later, the thrill of drinking my whole bottle of Coca-Cola hit me, and I needed to use the facilities. I started to get up when Mamo went into one of her snoring fits. It was so loud it woke her up, so I thought. She sat straight up in the bed, pointing her finger, whooping, and hollering at people I couldn't see and saying they had better get out of her house, or she was gonna shoot. I guess whoever it was didn't believe her, because Mamo started pointing her finger and shooting. When Mamo started shooting with her finger there was no doubt in my mind it was loaded, and if I moved the wrong way, Mamo could shoot me dead. As Mamo lowered her finger, I slowly rolled down into the bed. For the next thirty minutes I laid there in pain. Finally, Mamo got up and went into the kitchen. I ran to the bathroom that had the flushing toilet and, believe you me, that flush got its money's worth.

I tried to sneak back to bed cause the sun wasn't even up, but Mamo spied me. Mamo had this game she played with you. She called you the name of every relative dead or alive. Mamo started calling out "Debbie, Sheila, Katherine, Tammy, Susie, Marie, Trisha, Linda." Another game she played was whatever name she called you the most, even if it wasn't your name, was now your name. Linda was what Mamo called me, so when I heard that name I knew I had to go into the kitchen.

We started making the cinnamon bread. It was wonderful! Mamo didn't have the recipe written down. It was all in her head. She showed me what a handful was, what a pinch was, what a smidgen was, and what a dash was. She was about to show me how much yeast to put in when the phone rang. I don't know what came over me, but I was feeling like such a real girl. I could feel my cheeks glowing. I just knew I could put in the yeast all by myself. I put in a handful of yeast and started pullin' and pushin' that dough. Why, I was kneading dough like dough had never been kneaded. Mamo came back, and I told her I already put in the yeast. She said, "Oh ya did, did ya?" With a big smile I said, "Yes ma'am I sure did." We put the bread into the roasting pan and set it outside to rise in the warmth of the sun.

We returned to the house to fix breakfast for the rest of the sleepy heads. We cooked hog jaw, ham, bacon, sausage, fried eggs, fried taters, grits, gravy, biscuits, fried chicken, and fried tomatoes. I called out to my family that it was time to eat. One by one they came into the kitchen and took their place around the table. As we were eating, Mamo told them how I helped cook the breakfast and helped her make the cinnamon bread. No one said anything. They all just ate in silence, occasionally glancing at each other as though they expected something to happen.

After breakfast, it was time to check on my bread. Mamo said, "Y'all come look at Linda's bread." We marched out two by two with me and Mamo leading the way. We were about twenty feet away. I imagined how perfectly smooth and round it was going to look. We were ten feet away. I could just smell it and taste the homemade butter that would be poured all over the warm bread. We got about five feet away when we heard this giant "KABOOM!" The lid flew twenty-five feet into the air. It did three loops right and three loops to the left, landing in Miss Pallard's prize rose garden. Mother went through her "Oh Lordy, Lordy" routine. Debbie and Sheila started snickering. Dad, well… he just got the shovels. Mamo looked over at me, winked, and said, "Reckon my yeast just wantn' any good."

Everyone helped pick up the exploded cinnamon bread, then returned to the house to clean up the mess from breakfast. When we finished cleaning up, Mamo pointed to the high back chairs. We knew what that meant. We got the chairs and put them in a semi-circle around the radio. There we listened to the death reports as a way for us to calm down after such an exciting morning.

Chapter Three - Visiting Trips with Mamo

After calming down from listening to the death reports on the radio, we all went about our day. Dad, Mom, and Sheila went to Lawrenceburg to visit with our country grandparents, Ma and Pa Coats.

Debbie and I stayed with Mamo to accompany her on her visiting trips. We watched her get ready as she sat on her padded baroque bench in front of her mirror and opened the drawer to her right, where she kept her makeup. She put on a little powder, a little rouge, and a little bit of red lipstick. Not too much, because Mamo didn't want to look like a brazen hussy. Debbie and I didn't know what that meant, but we liked the sound of it, brazen hussy.

The reason we liked saying it so much was because we knew we could only get away with saying it at Mamo's house, as mother didn't like that word. When we said it, her eyes rolled to the back of her head, going down to her heels and toes, then back up to her eye sockets. They were a color we had never seen before.

When Mamo finished her make-up, she pulled open the drawer on the left to fix her hair. She always pulled it into a bun on top of her head, placing a hair net around the bun. She had to make sure that her bangs were fixed a certain way. Mamo had something on her forehead that she called a knot. It looked like a gumball in the middle of her forehead. She didn't want anyone to look at her knot, so she spent time to make sure it was covered.

I don't know how Mamo got the knot. I just know she always had her knot. Debbie and I used to think that when Mamo didn't have to be Mamo, she was a unicorn, and when we came to visit her, not all of her would fit into her body, and the knot was left.

Mamo handed Debbie and me the keys to open the shed door. The shed was a big white wooden building with two doors. We unlocked the door on the left. It took both of us to slide the door open. The dirt floors had a musty smell. The walls were decorated with food Mamo had canned for the winter. On the left side was the green two-tone Ford. Mamo's everyday car. It had a big round steering wheel with a small glass knob on the top that Mamo used instead of the steering wheel to drive the car. She looked a little bit like she was driving a semi-truck.

Our first stop was Aunt Janey's house. She wasn't much taller than Debbie and me. She let us look through her picture viewfinder while she served iced tea in her mason jars. In her gentle southern drawl, she told us how polite we were and what little ladies we were and asked our ages. Debbie said she was eleven going on twelve This year I got to say twelve going on thirteen. Mamo leaned over to us and said, "No need to tell someone what you're goin' on cause people already know, 'sides a lady never tells any more of her age than she has ta." We didn't mind playing Mamo's lady games. We knew her wild side.

After three more, "Honey child, I almost died!" visits we went to our last one, Miss Smith. Debbie and I were really glad Miss Smith wasn't dead. She was the funniest, sickest lady we ever knew. Miss Smith had the misery. She took a lot of medicine during the day. She didn't have to use a spoon like Debbie and me. She got to drink hers right out of a brown jug that had a little spout on top and a hook on the side. We were always amazed how she could put her finger in the hook, hold it sideways to her mouth, drink from it, and never spill a drop. Sometimes her medicine made her a little dizzy, and we picked her up when she fell off her chair.

After several falls, Mamo said it was time for us to leave as we needed to fix supper. Again, I was the only one who got to help Mamo. Supper consisted of ham, cornbread, pinto beans, turnip greens, cucumbers and onions, and chess pie.

Chapter Four - Hanging out with Mamo

After cleaning up from dinner, Mamo told Debbie and me she would take us to the places where there were young people. We got ourselves ready, while Mamo freshened her rouge, powder, and lipstick, not too much because Mamo didn't want to look like a brazen hussy. While she was fixing her bangs to cover up her knot, she gave us the keys to the shed again.

This time we slid the door open on the right side. The smell of the dirt floor was stronger after the short rain that fell during the night. The walls on this side were also decorated with Mamo's canned goods. The Mercury, Mamo's going out for the evening car, was parked on this side. It was huge, white, and had a button to push to make the window go up and down. Debbie and I each got a turn to make our windows go up and down. If I worked it exactly right, I got two turns. I pushed my button to make the window go down, leaned out the window, and looked really scared. I'd tell Debbie there were footprints on the ground and they looked like they belonged to Bigfoot. I told her not to look but, you know, by the time baby sisters are born there aren't any smart brain cells left. As Debbie was looking out the window, I pushed my button to make my window go up, getting her head stuck in the window. Mamo slightly looked back and said, "Linda, let yourn sister's head back into the car." I pushed my button again to make it go down, so I could get Debbie's head out of the window. I got two turns.

What Mamo liked to do most in the Mercury was cruise for boys. She pulled up to a stop sign next to a car load of boys, pushed her button to make her window go down and yelled, "These here are my granddaughters. Wanna race?" Mamo revved up her motor and peeled off at a top speed of 30 mph. Mamo always won. I'm quite sure it was because the boys were still at the stop sign with a puzzled look on their faces.

After cruising, we went to the bowling alley. While Debbie and I were bowling, Mamo was picking up boys. We heard her say, "These here are my granddaughters from Illinois." She gently guided them to the lane where we were bowling. We were only allowed to talk to the boys Mamo picked up, and we weren't allowed to talk to them very long. Mamo didn't think we ought to be engaged that summer. She didn't think our mother would approve.

Our last stop was our favorite place to go, the skating rink. Before we went to the rink, we had to pick up Mamo's friend, Mary. Mary was a nice lady. Mary's husband, Jimmy, was hard of hearing. Mary thought everyone else was hard of hearing, so she talked real loud. The louder she talked, the faster she talked. The faster she talked, the louder she talked. Debbie and I couldn't wait to get to the skating rink because it was a lot quieter there than the ride in the car with Mamo's friend, Mary.

While Debbie and I were skating, we saw Mamo picking up boys, and pushing them onto the floor. When she had rounded up a few, she sat on the bench at the side of the rink. If she didn't think any boys were paying any attention to us, she would stand up, point and holler "These here are my granddaughters from Illinois. Y'all go skate with 'em." Sometimes Mamo got so wound up in picking up the boys on the skating floor she didn't notice there was a fast song playing. Her head moved around and around the rink trying to follow the boys as fast as the song was playing. Before you knew it, she lost her balance, and fell back onto the bench. We heard Mamo's friend, Mary, above all the music yelling, "Ellie Mai, you're gonna plum lose your head one day." Mary helped Mamo get her wits about her, and made sure her bangs were exactly right so no one could see her knot.

Chapter Five - Mamo's Secret Ingredient

In 1974 Mamo was diagnosed with leukemia. The thought of dying didn't bother her, for she was prepared to meet her Maker. But the thought of losing all her hair through chemotherapy meant people would see her knot, and that terrified her. By this time, Debbie had finished beauty school. She sent Mamo wigs in every shade of red with bangs that covered the knot.

Two years later, Mamo died. Friends and relatives came to pay their respects. Before the minister conducted the funeral service, everyone sang "The Old Rugged Cross" and "In the Sweet By and By." After the minister finished, the funeral director started to close the lid of the casket. Something caught everyone's eyes. We were slowly bending from the waist following the lid as it was being closed to see if we were really seeing what we thought we saw. Mamo's wig was all the way down to her nose! I thought Mamo would just die if she could see her wig.

Then I remembered where I was. I guess what happened was those who knew how Mamo felt about that knot, gave her wig a little tug as they passed by the casket, not realizing how much it would move. We all covered up our mouths with our hands while our bodies shook up and down trying to keep the laughter inside, but it was of no use.

Laughter filled the funeral home. But you see, that's how Mamo was. She always left you with a laugh, and to me laughter is the only ingredient needed to be... a real girl.

Sarah Jane

Chapter One - The Store

Sarah Jane lived in a small farming community in Tennessee known as Center Town because it was located in the heart of all the farms. Sarah Jane's parents owned a general store where all the town folk gathered to socialize.

Men came to buy farming supplies and swap stories around the old potbelly stove. The women sorted through the dry goods and leafed through the mail order catalog to catch a glimpse of what the city folks were wearing. The children drooled over the penny candy, hoping their mama or daddy would buy them some. Sarah Jane always sat at the front of the store in the chair that her daddy made for her so she could see the folks coming and going.

There was something special about Sarah Jane. She couldn't walk or talk. Her arms and legs were twisted. Someone had to dress her, feed her, and bathe her. Someone had to make sure she was moved around so she wouldn't get sores on her body. She could do nothing for herself. No one knew why she was born that way, but to folks from Center Town it didn't matter. That is what made her special.

Everyone who came into the store took the time to talk to Sarah Jane. Even though she could not respond, they knew she was listening. Some of the farmers would even ask for her advice, "Sarah Jane, what do ya think about them crops? I reckon we just ain't gonna have a good one this year." Sarah Jane would look up at them and smile as though to say, "It'll be alright." For some unknown reason, the farmers felt at peace and knew their crops would be fine.

Will Coats came into the store to let the folks know the Long family needed help to build a barn. Folks were always willing to help someone build a barn, and the summer was a good time to build it before the crops were ready for harvest. After the barn was built, all who helped enjoyed going to the barn raising party.

Chapter Two - Getting Ready for the Party

The folks from Center Town finished the barn just before it was time for the harvest. There was so much to do before the party that night. The men folk were setting up bales of hay for sitting, securing wood onto saw horses for tables, lanterns spread out for light, and a stage for the band. The women folk were cooking pies, bread, and roasting a hog. The children were running around playing tag while trying to sneak a bite or two of the pies.

When the preparations were finished, everyone returned home to get all gussied up for the party.

Sarah Jane's mama fixed her long dark brown hair into flowing banana curls. She placed a pink bow on each side of her head, just above her ears, which matched her Sunday goin' to meetin' clothes.

While Sarah Jane waited to go to the party, her daddy hitched the horses to the wagon. Her mama packed the back of the wagon with the picnic basket full of food and Sarah Jane's chair. When all was in place daddy went to the house and picked up Sarah Jane. As he carried her to the wagon, he carefully held her so not to cause her any pain

He placed her next to him in the wagon seat, making sure there was no way for her to fall. He held the reins, moving them to slightly hit the back of the horses while making a clicking noise that signaled the horses to move. Off to the barn raising party they went.

Chapter Three - At the Party

They arrived at the party and unloaded the back of the wagon. Sarah Jane's daddy gently carried her inside the barn to her chair that was up front, next to those playing the music for the night. This way she could see everything and everyone. Harley played the spoons, Susie played the washboard, and her Uncle Slim played the fiddle. Some folks were doing the Virginia Reel. Some were doing a jig. There was nonstop dancing, singing, and laughing.

When it was time for everyone to catch their breath, a slow song was played. Sarah Jane's Uncle Slim took his fiddle to play her favorite song. He called it The Night Waltz. He knew it was her favorite, for whenever he played it, she looked right at him and her eyes lit up. Sarah Jane made noises that made no distinctive words, but her Uncle Slim knew she was singing while he played his fiddle. Everyone watched as Sarah Jane tried so hard to sing and move her twisted body to the rhythm of the song. Folks stopped their dancing so as to give her "the floor." A tear found itself in the eye of even the biggest man there as he watched her try to dance.

The thing Sarah Jane loved most about these parties was the game she played while listening to the Night Waltz. She closes her eyes and pretends she is at the party walking, talking, and dancing. She no longer has to be carried. She does everything for herself. A fine, tall, handsome, young man dressed in his best Sunday overalls walks over to her, stumbling over his words, as he shyly asks, "Sarah Jane, wooodcha like to dance with me?" She takes out her fan, as all ladies have one, fanning herself while gently curtsying and replies, "Why sir, I would be most honored to dance with you." He takes her hand, guiding her to the middle of the floor where they dance. Sarah Jane never stopped dancing. She was in heaven on earth.

Chapter Four - Awakened from the Dream

Sarah Jane's dream was interrupted by someone shouting, "Fire! Fire! There's a fire in the barn! Let the animals loose! Start the bucket brigade!" The thick black smoke filled the barn so fast it was impossible to see anything or anyone. The intense heat from the flames made it hard for the bucket brigade to get anywhere near the barn. A loud shout came from outside, "Get out! It's a comin' down!"

All they could do was watch the barn burn. Any efforts to save it were in vain. Their dress clothes were torn and smelled of smoke. Some were attending to those who had burns and those who had inhaled smoke. Exhausted, they tried to comfort each other as they sat in silence.

A voice filled with despair broke the silence, "Sarah? Sarah! Have you seen my Sarah Jane?" Folks could only shake their heads no, feeling sick of what they dreaded might have happened. With all the confusion of trying to get out of the barn through the heat and smoke, each one thought

24

someone had picked up Sarah Jane. Sadly, no one had gotten her out of the barn.

Chapter Five - The Night Waltz

A few weeks later, folks gathered to clean up the remains trying to salvage anything that could help rebuild the barn. The harvest was coming, and the Long family needed a barn.

While they were working, something strange happened. Every time a piece of wood was picked up, they heard music. They tried to ignore it, but the music wouldn't stop. It got louder. They stopped to listen and soon recognized it to be the Night Waltz. The song that made Sarah Jane happy.

They looked at each other and at Sarah Jane's parents crying. The folks of Center Town agreed never to rebuild the barn.

To those who didn't know Sarah Jane, it looks like a heap of old burned rubble, but to the folks of Center Town, it is alive with the treasured memory of Sarah Jane.

It is said that to this day when there is a soft autumn breeze you can hear the music of the Night Waltz coming from the pile, and if it is a full moon you can see Sarah Jane dancing and dancing and dancing.

The barn was never rebuilt, and Sarah Jane was never forgotten.

When we took our yearly trip to Tennessee, we stopped in Lawrenceburg to visit Ma and Pa Coats. Neither one of them drove a car, so when they needed groceries or supplies, Pa Coats would hook up the wagon to his tractor and make a trip to Center Town. As a child, I thought this was the neatest thing on earth. Sitting in the back of a wagon, waving to people, anticipating purchasing the red jello and bananas that Ma Coats let me make.

The owners of the store did have a daughter with a disability. I did not know what it was, but I did see the way she was treated by those coming into the store. She was accepted in a time when that was not the norm. I looked forward to seeing her each year when we traveled to Center Town.

I Got A Whoopin'

Chapter One - The Middle Child

Debbie is my younger sister. I am her elder by eighteen months. Sheila is my older sister by five years. You probably figured out I am the middle child. The one that is just there. I did try to make myself known, but it usually wasn't in the most positive way. Sheila wouldn't let me hang around her as I might use up the same air she was breathing. Debbie liked dolls, having her hair fixed, and everyone just went "Ga Ga and Goo Goo" over her. I, on the other hand, was a tomboy. My mother's worst nightmare come to life.

Since Sheila forbade me to hang with her, I was stuck with Debbie. I had to include her in all that I did, I gave her life experiences to expand her horizons. I exposed her to elements that would enhance her potential to the fullest. I added excitement to what would have been a very boring childhood for her. At least that's the way I saw it. My mother saw it as something short of putting me in a home for wayward girls.

Chapter Two - Expanding Debbie's Horizons

On Saturdays, while our parents were at work, we had to clean the whole house before we could play. Being inside was not for me. I lived to be outside.

Debbie lived to sleep. When she did arise, she went to the refrigerator, got a bowl of ice cream, and crumbled a Twinkie into it. Then she went into the living room and sat in an orange swivel chair with plastic on it, that only came off for company, and watched cartoons on our black and white television.

I tried to reason with her week after week, but it was of no use. One Saturday, I had enough. I was using the Electrolux vacuum. When I saw Debbie was still asleep on the bottom bunk I noticed she had one foot uncovered, just hanging over the end of the bed. I looked at her big toe, looked at the vacuum, and then back to her big toe. I took off the attachment and crammed her big toe into the hose. She let out a high-pitched scream while trying to get out of the bed. The combination of her rolling around and the fact that her toe was bigger than the hose opening, which explains why I had such a hard time shoving her toe in, created a super-duper suction. She fell to the floor with one leg draped on top of the bed and her toe still attached to the hose.

Now, you would have thought that mother and father knew that I knew that the wooden spindle footboard would stop the vacuum from coming completely over on Debbie and possibly killing her.

But, they did not see it that way and, needless to say, I got a whoopin' that night.

Every time I went to play with my friends I had to take Darling Debbie along, or I couldn't go. One-time we girls were at Julie Ann's house. They all wanted to dress up, which was not my thing. However, Sherry had her mom's old Wave uniform from when she was in the Navy. I could wear this and save face when I played ball with the boys. But Debbie took the uniform. I really didn't mind that so much, for my eye caught something else at the bottom of the box. It was white. It was huge. It looked like two balls had been cut in half. Those halves were side by side and connected with wires running through the bottom. The top part was standing out all by itself. It would be the perfect double barrel slingshot. I started to get it out of the box when Debbie grabbed my slingshot. She said she had to wear it under her uniform top to make her look pretty. I wanted to throw up.

When she had on a skirt and my slingshot, I grabbed all her clothes and ran outside, daring her to chase me. Baby sisters aren't too smart. She came running after me, yelling how she was going to tell mom if I didn't give her back her clothes. I turned around to see her angry little face when I fell to the ground laughing. Every time Debbie ran, my beautiful slingshot was hitting her in the face. It caused the most wonderful nosebleed! Blood was squirting in every direction.

Now, you would have thought that mother and father took into consideration that I helped stop Debbie's nose bleed. But, they did not see it that way and, needless to say, I got a whoopin' that night.

I loved to cut the grass, especially with our brand-new Roper riding lawn mower. Debbie had to have gloves on top of her gloves if she ever did any yard work, so I knew she would never want to cut the grass. It was mine, all mine. But since it was a rider, she now wanted to cut the grass. She kept whining and crying and carrying on until she got her way. Dad told me I had to teach her how to use my riding lawn mower.

She climbed onto my lawn mower with such a snot nose grin I felt it my duty to remove it. I told her that after I started it to keep her eye on the pedal and to pay no attention to the steering wheel because it was only decoration. I told her when I said go to push the pedal down all the way to the floor. I then put it into third gear and yelled, "Go!"

Now, you would have thought that mother and father knew that I knew when Debbie and the tree met, the mower would stop. But, they didn't see it that way and, needless to say, I got a whoopin' that night.

Chapter Three - We Grew Up

As adults the miles have separated us, but our hearts have never been separated. Our childhood helped us gain a sixth sense in knowing when the other is in need. When that feeling is strong, the phone rings.

We've shared in each other's happiness such as our marriages, her promotion, my starting my own preschool, our new homes, the relationship she has with her stepchildren, the birth of my children, and her being the doting aunt.

We've shared in each other's grief such as the night her youngest stepson was in a coma from a car accident, the stress of her job, my feeling like I had let God down when I couldn't reach our foster children, and the emptiness she felt when she was unable to carry a child to term, so desperately wanting just one child. The only thing I could do was hold her and cry along with her. She had done this with me when I thought we wouldn't have any children.

Debbie is a second mother to my children, and I couldn't be prouder. She may not ever be able to have children of her own while living here on

31

earth. Yet, I have faith that when we are in heaven she will have children sitting all around her, just glued to the wonderful stories she has to tell about living with a loving, strong-willed, but ever so creative older sister who, needless to say - always got a whoopin'.

After I put this story together, Debbie found out she was pregnant. She and her husband John had a little girl named Kelsey Mai. Her middle name is the same middle name of her favorite aunt - me. Kelsey and her husband are expecting their first child in November 2020. They will be having a little boy. He is to be named after a great man, my father, and her grandfather. He will be called Oliver.

The Witch

I grew up in Kankakee, Illinois, out in the country, in a subdivision called Skyline. There was a row of seven houses. If you added up the number of children living in them, it came to twenty-two of us. We all rode our bikes together, played a game of piggy-at-work at any given moment, or gathered around a campfire making up stories about the witch who lived two houses away from ours with her son and daughter-in-law, known as Uncle Finley and Aunt Sarah.

Chapter One - Skyline

Every morning at 10:00, we hid in the bushes by the side of the witch's house, waiting for her to come outside onto the front porch. She slowly opened the door and looked all around. Not seeing whatever she was looking for, she walked over to her broom that was propped up in the corner. She always wore a long black dress. Her white hair was pulled tightly off her face and twisted into a bun on the back of her head. We watched patiently hoping to see her fly, but she never did. She moved around and around with the broom to the beat of her chants. We couldn't make out the words, but we knew they were witch words. She was probably conjuring up some kind of spell. She always seemed to know we were there, for she would stop, stare at the bushes with those piercing eyes, and chant. Our hearts were beating so loud, we just knew she heard us. She stepped off the porch to walk toward us, but we all ran as fast as we could to get away from her. She never caught us.

Sometimes when we were feeling the power of our lucky rabbit's foot, we played a game when she was outside with her broom. We drew blades of grass, and the shortest one ran across her yard and then back to the bushes before she put a spell on us. If you returned in less than two minutes you got to be a captain for the baseball game we played later that day.

Whenever someone ran across her yard, she froze like a statue at the courthouse. The only thing moving was her piercing eyes. When it was Donnie's turn to run across, we hoped he didn't make it back to the bushes. He was the neighborhood bully.

The grownups said the witch was just a lonely old lady, but we knew her powers. She made Colleen's family move to California. The grownups said her dad got a transfer. She made Debbie Ann's throat get so infected she had to go to the hospital for surgery. The grownups said she had her tonsils removed. She made my sister Debbie and me get red bumps all over our bodies. The grownups said we had the measles. We knew better than the grownups and just waited for the right moment to prove them wrong.

Chapter Two - The Meeting

The witch's powers were getting stronger. They were taking control of my mother. She was like a zombie walking around, only able to say, "Yes, Master." Aunt Sarah and Uncle Finley were going camping for the weekend, and they needed someone to stay with the witch. My mother volunteered me! Now, it's true at twelve years of age, I was somewhat of a strong-willed child, but I did nothing that deserved being eaten alive. Unless you count the time I took my jacket and hit Sherry in the mouth with the zipper, causing her to bleed for twenty minutes - like I knew my zipper was ripped and sticking out. Or the time I took tar off the road and put it down John Otterly's back and rubbed his shirt into the black goo. I should have received an awarded for that since he was a bigger bully than Donnie. I begged mother over and over not to make me go, but she kept saying, "It'll be alright. It'll be alright," as she laughed in an eerie sort of way.

I called a meeting of all the kids and told them what happened. They couldn't believe I had to actually be in the house with the witch by myself all night long. I told them that since the witch's powers were getting so strong and taking over the neighborhood, there was only one thing that I could do. I had to get into the house to find the source of her power to break the spell she had over everyone. It was up to me. Just in case I didn't return, I gave my softball to Kenny, my Barbie doll to Linda, my Dick Tracey decoder watch to Sherry, and my baseball cards to Mike. Then I left.

Chapter Three - The Night with the Witch

The night came for me to meet the hardest challenge I ever had to encounter. I knew I was going up against forces much stronger than mine, but I was prepared to die, die for my country if necessary. This evil force had to be destroyed.

I went over to my family to kiss them goodbye. They were sitting around our black and white television. that swirled from side to side, watching "Sing Along with Mitch." Their heads bobbed up and down as they followed the bouncing ball on top of the words to the song. They were oblivious to what I was going to do for them. I walked out like a soldier going off to war, never looking back at my family. I wanted to remember them just as they were. So carefree. So trusting.

I arrived at the witch's house that night promptly at 7:00. Aunt Sarah took me around the house, giving me instructions of what had to be done and a list of emergency numbers. Like I was really going to get to use them.

As they drove off, I felt like I was the only person in the world. I accepted that I may never be seen or heard from again. I was totally helpless, but totally committed.

Chapter Four - The Memory

The living room was dark and full of smells of burning candles. The witch sat in a faded floral chair, with dingy white crocheted scarves on the arms and back of the chair. The witch motioned with her hand for me to sit in the big, black, overstuffed chair. I sat quietly, looking around, trying to find an escape route in case I needed one.

The witch slowly got up from her chair and went into the kitchen. She returned with a glass of cherry Kool-Aid. Should I drink it or not? I knew there had to be poison in the glass. Yet, If I was to die, this would be a good way to go. Besides, I was really thirsty. I drank the Kool-Aid. Nothing happened!

She returned to the kitchen. This time she brought back a plate of homemade chocolate chip cookies. Her powers to reel in her victims were good. How did she know these were my favorite kind of cookies? Should I eat them or not? I knew there had to be poison in them. Yet, if I was going to die this would be a good way to go. Besides, I was really hungry. I ate the cookies. Nothing happened!

The night went on with us glancing and smiling at each other, not saying a word. She turned on the television and waited for it warm up to see what was on the screen. I recognized the show. It was one we watched every week because it was my dad's favorite, The Rat Patrol. I sat glued to the black chair, watching the show, and fighting along with our guys to victory.

I happened to glance over at her and noticed a single tear running down the witch's face. I wanted to ask her what was wrong, but I knew it was a witch trick. Another single tear came down her face. She tried to hide it, but I could see right through her. Then, more tears came. I went against all my Saturday morning training I learned from watching Dick Tracy, Huckleberry Hound, and Scooby-Doo. I looked her straight in the eyes to ask her what was wrong. I had to listen very carefully, as she spoke differently than I ever heard anyone speak. Her words were not what I expected to hear.

"Zis movie remind me of ven I vass little girl yourz age. I levee in Auztria. My papa waz taylerr. I help him in zore. Ve ver happy, but outzide zore timez vere not happy. Nazis zaking over townz and zake Jewz from zeir homez. I vas zo zare zey vould come to our zown. Papa knew thiz and vould calm my fearz by getzining ze broom. He play game vith me. Vhile zweeping the floor we danze and zing, to keep mindz off zrouble."

She slowly moved her hunched over body to get up from her chair to walk to the kitchen. She returned with her broom that barely had enough straw to clean up anything. Her feet slowly shuffled along the floor as she danced to the song she was singing. I watched for a couple of minutes. She reached out her hand and invited me to join her.

While we were dancing, I realized that when she was dancing and singing on the porch it was to make herself happy. She was not doing a witch ritual. She stopped her dancing to continue her story.

"De Nazis com to zee zore. Zey draz uz away. I zaken from my family, zoved into zruck, to camp. People beaten and ztarved. I was lucky vone. My faderer vas zailor and I know hez zrade. Zey needed officers' uniforms repaired and ztars sewn on clothes of Jews. Zewing kept me alive."

She rolled back her sleeve to show me numbers in her arms. I knew these were not like the tattoos we got out of the Cracker Jack Box. She took my hand and placed it on the numbers so I could feel them. I no longer feared her. I felt sorry for her. I admired her.

I snuggled up into my chair, glued to the stories she told of the things she did as a little girl in Austria. The last thing I remember was her covering me up as I fell asleep.

Chapter Five - The Game Changed

When I awoke the next morning, I wasn't sure if I was dreaming or if the night had really happened. The room was much brighter and more cheerful than when I arrived the night before. The flowers in her chair were a mix of pastel colors. The scarves on the back and each side of the chair were a bright white. There were little flowers on her black dress. Her white hair accented her eyes that were now full of life. They actually looked like they were still dancing.

Later that morning, Aunt Sarah and Uncle Finley came home. I reported that all went well and to feel free to call me anytime they went away. I went over to the witch to give her a hug and told her good-by. She patted me on the head and called me, Kliner. I remembered from her stories that meant, "my little one," a name her Papa called her.

I returned home, but now I had another problem. What was I going to tell the other kids? Do I let them go on thinking she's a witch? Do I tell them I found the source of her power and destroyed it? Or, do I tell them the truth? I called a meeting. Everyone came but Donnie. Our meeting was beneath him. I told them the truth. They hung on to my every word, as I had to hers the night before.

We hide in the bushes to wait for her to come out to the front porch, grab her broom, look at us as we run across the yard and back to the bushes. All but one of us knew she won't turn us into anything. We never told Donnie what really happened. We wanted him to believe she was still a witch and could put a spell on him. But for the rest of us, we made slight eye contact and give a small wave. She would say something back to us which we didn't understand, but that didn't matter. For that short time in her yard, we were doing what all children should do, simply playing.

Section Two - Teacher

I was a preschool teacher for twenty-five years, which I thoroughly loved. The children inspired me by the many things they said or did. As much as I loved teaching, I could be overwhelmed with day to day planning. Sometimes I doubted myself or lost sight of why I was teaching. I was blessed to have the children bring me back to the real world, their world. They were the inspiration for these songs and stories.

Sometimes I Wonder

Sometimes I wonder if what I'm doing is right.
Teaching little ones to soar to new heights.
Do they listen? Can they see
The potential of what they can be?

Then a child will show me what there needs to be.
If I only listen, then their world I'll see.
She stretches out her hand and gives to me
Reminders of what a child needs to be.

A picture painting blue.
Lines say I love you,
A bug that should be flyin'
And a bouquet of dandelions.

The picture is hung on our gallery of fame,
Then we go outside, play our favorite game.
"Teacher, I love you," she shouts across the room,
Waves goodbye, "I'll see you soon."

The bug in my hand is lying oh so still.
Then it flies off, and we all give a squeal.
Teacher close your eyes and hold your hand,
Then I feel the flowers oh so grand.

Oh, I know what I'm doing is right.
Teaching little ones to soar to new heights.
Yes, they listen. Yes, they see,
The potential of what they can be.

For a child will show me what there needs to be.
If I only listen, then their world I'll see.
She stretches out her hand and gives to me
Reminders of what a child needs to be.

A picture painting blue.
Lines say I love you,
A bug that should be flyin'
And a bouquet of dandelions.

Teacher, Teacher

In the early years of my teaching my written lesson plans would please any administrator. But there were times when something unexpected happened and it became an amazing lesson. There were also times when a child had a heart wrenching question that would never be in a lesson plan. I discovered that I needed help from the greatest teacher I knew in order to be prepared for whatever I encountered that day. From that realization came this song.

Teacher, Teacher, why don't the clouds fall?
Why don't the fish drown?
Why won't my friend play with me?
And why don't mommy and daddy live in the same house?

The lesson is planned for the day.
It'll be numbers, letters, and shapes.
Will I teach so they understand?
A helicopter goes by, so we run out to fly along.

Teacher, Teacher, why don't the clouds fall?
Why don't the fish drown?
Why won't my friend play with me?
And why don't mommy and daddy live in the same
house?

The lesson is planned for the day.
It'll be story, music, and art.
Will I teach so they understand?
A woodpecker's beak gets caught in our screen, and
we feel its pain.

Teacher, Teacher, why don't the clouds fall?
Why don't the fish drown?
Why won't my friend play with me?
And why don't mommy and daddy live in the same
house?

The lesson is planned for the day.
It'll be science, colors, and math.
Will I teach so they understand?
A little one cries because his mother has left, so we
share a hug.

Teacher, Teacher, why don't the clouds fall?
Why don't the fish drown?
Why won't my friend play with me?
And why don't mommy and daddy live in the same
house?

The lesson is planned for the day.
How do I cover all that they need?
With the most important being self-worth?
But all becomes easier when I kneel before the
loving teacher above.

Teacher, Teacher, why don't the clouds fall?
Why don't the fish drown?
Why won't my friend play with me?
And why don't mommy and daddy live in the same
house?

Little Lessons of Life

Throughout my twenty-five years as a preschool teacher I heard the same three questions asked every day. I soon realized the importance of addressing them every day, several times a day.

Today is the first day of preschool.
I was the teacher, oh so cool.
They kissed their moms goodbye.
A few of them did cry.
But then they turned to me, and they said.

Are we going outside?
Are we gonna have snacks?
And when is my mother coming back?
For teacher you must know,
This is what makes us go.
These little lessons of life, they are gold.

The next time they came, I went to plan "B."
I brought in leaves from different trees.
Maple, Elm, and Oak oh
Something to tell their folks,
But then they turned to me and they said.

Are we going outside?
Are we gonna have snacks?
And when is my mother coming back?
For teacher you must know,
This is what makes us go.
These little lessons of life, they are gold.

The next time they came, I went to plan "O."
Doing experiments with the snow.
Did it feel cold or hot?
Now look into the pot.
But then they turned to me and they said.

Are we going outside?
Are we gonna have snacks?
And when is my mother coming back?
For teacher you must know,
This is what makes us go.
These little lessons of life, they are gold.

The next time they came, I went to plan "T."
Numbers, letters, and stories all about spring.
Playdough, bubbles, and cars.
Oh, I wanted to take them far,
But then they turned to me and they said.

Are we going outside?
Are we gonna have snacks?
And when is my mother coming back?

For teacher you must know,
This is what makes us go.
These little lessons of life, they are gold.

I finally saw what had to be the plan.
All I had to do was join their band.
With the music from each child.
Imaginations sang wild.
So I turned to them and I said.

Yes! we're going outside.
Yes! we're gonna have snacks.
And your mother will soon be back.
For as a teacher I must know.
This is what makes you go.
These little lessons of life, they are gold.

Don't Interrupt

Several of us went to a local restaurant Sunday morning after church. My attention was drawn to the table in front of me as they were singing "Happy Birthday." Sitting at the table was a woman I recognized named Ami, for her child Abby attended my preschool, Special Friends. I didn't go over to the table, as I didn't want to disturb their celebration. Rather, we waved and smiled to acknowledge each other.

I turned back to the conversation at our table, never noticing Ami leaving. I felt a hand on my shoulder and turned to see who it was. It was Ami. She said her niece wanted to talk to me but was told not to interrupt my lunch. Her niece started to cry and could not be consoled, which is why Ami came to me to see if it was okay to bring her over. My heart sank when I heard this. I told her to please let her come to the table.

As she was coming over, I recognized this beautiful child as one of my former preschoolers, Mia. I hadn't seen her earlier while listening to them all singing, but now we had our time. I loved visiting with her and hearing all that was going on with her. When she was through sharing, we gave each other one more big hug before saying good-bye.

When we were leaving the restaurant, a couple in the booth behind us stopped me to tell me they had seen what happened with the little girl and were so happy she was allowed to talk with me. Of course, I took the opportunity to tell them about the joys of being a preschool teacher and how blessed I was to have my own preschool, called "Special Friends."

We teach our children not to interrupt adults when they are speaking, as we should. But I'm so thankful Mia didn't see it as interrupting me that day, for we were just special friends talking.

Section Three - Be Still

How many of us ever told a child to be still? Fidgeting is not only directed to children. It can happen to adults, especially those of us who are a little high strung, even without a pot or two of coffee.

I have found the times when I do slow down and actually stop to breathe, God is there.

The writings in this section of the book came from the times I was in the moment and remembered the words from Psalm 46:10:

Be still and know that I am God.

Half Empty or Half Full

According to Wikipedia, "Is the glass half empty or half full?" is a common expression, a proverbial phrase, generally used rhetorically to indicate that a particular situation could be a cause for optimism (half full) or pessimism (half empty).

To give it more clarity, a person who is optimistic tends to take a favorable view of events or conditions and to expect the most favorable outcome; while a person who is pessimistic tends to see the worst aspect of things or believe that the worst will happen.

I tend to lean more optimistic; but there are times I dwell on being pessimistic, and there are times I tend to be more "gripeimistic." Gripeimistic will never be found in Wikipedia or any medical book. I made up the name.

When I am gripeimistic I do not see the glass half empty or half full, but rather see something wrong with the glass, what's inside the glass, where the glass was purchased, the person who purchased the glass, the person who put whatever inside the glass, get upset with having the same thing in the glass, get upset when putting something different into the glass, wanting whatever is inside the glass at the same level, get upset if it's too high or too low. In other words, there is just no pleasing me.

Now, don't get me wrong. At times I believe we all need a "Two Minute Pity Party." It is when I dwell on self-pity I find myself becoming sad, which turns to anger and not caring who I bring down with me.

Not only can I be gripeimistic in my everyday life, I can bring it to my spiritual life. I do not see the church as half empty or half full; rather I see something wrong with the church, who is at church, who isn't at church, the songs that were sung, the songs that weren't sung, sermons that were preached, the sermons that weren't preached, the lessons being taught, the lessons not taught, the outreach that is being done, the outreach that isn't being done, upset with those who don't volunteer for anything but I wouldn't volunteer myself. Again, there is just no pleasing me, and the only thing I do is tear down the church.

I don't pretend to be any type of medical authority on these real or made up "imitics." Here are some suggestions that have helped me:

> I confide in someone I trust not to repeat my rantings. There is a fine line between griping and venting. Griping makes me look good by tearing everyone else down. Venting helps me put things into perspective and is a stress reliever.

Sometimes my venting requires that I swallow my pride, especially when I realize I'm part of the problem.

➢ I must separate myself from whoever or whatever is pulling me down by doing something that requires physical activity, which I try to do outside. Something about seeing God's nature and exhausting my body to release those endorphins feels so good. (If exercising is not your thing, dark chocolate will work.)

➢ Volunteer to help change whatever I'm griping about by reminding myself I am here to serve, not to be served. I need to put up or shut up.

➢ Give myself permission to be happy. Happiness is not a sign of weakness.

➢ For every negative , I must come up with two positives.

Luckily for us, God doesn't have to come up with a plan. His love for us is never half empty or half full. His glass runs over and never runs out.

Blow Your Horn

The other day as I was leaving a store, I heard children yelling, "Blow your horn!" I stopped to see what was going on when I saw arms bent at the elbow, hands held high in a fist while moving them all up and down in one movement. Then they started squealing in laughter, clapping their hands, and jumping up and down as the semi slowly passed them sounding its horn.

I recalled a memory of my parents showing my sisters and me how to do this when passing semis on our yearly road trips to Tennessee. Keeping the tradition, I showed this to my children, who in turn showed it to their children.

In the weeks prior, the news was filled with reports of children shooting each other, starving, being bullied, on drugs, being sold, and parents killing children. It was so refreshing to see these children clapping, jumping, and yelling in excitement when the horn was blown.

My heart ached for children who had no youth. "Why wasn't anyone looking out for them? What kind of family life did they have? Why didn't God step in and stop this?"

I would give my views while sitting with friends having coffee, but that's not going to change anything. On occasions, I donated and worked with organizations that help children in distress.

So, What Can I Do?

As simple as this sounds, I encourage parents to just play with their children. Play doesn't care if both parents are in the home, or it is a single-parent home, no matter where you live, no matter what your income, no matter what your race. Play is non-judgmental. Play is universal.

But play isn't as easy as it sounds, because children need to be taught how to play without a screen in front of them. I used to think this should be directed to just parents, but I am seeing more and more of us grandparents glued to a screen. This means all adults must put away their cell phones and laptops, and turn off the television. We should never just give a slight glance to acknowledge them. Children need our full attention.

So, what do you do if you can't have a screen in front of you? Simple. Jump in a mud puddle, make mud cakes, look for "tropical fish" in the creek, ride a bike, go for a walk, look for animal shapes in the clouds, bake making the biggest mess you can, color, play flashlight tag using a real flashlight not the one on your phone, dress up in old clothes, put on a play, snuggle while reading a real book not an electronic one, make up stories, crafts, or come up with ideas on your own. No googling. Use your imagination.

Whatever ideas you come up with help keep this tradition of playing alive. Show a child how to make a truck blow its horn. Then, do it one more time for that little one who was never allowed to be a child.

APD

I know prayer is talking with God, it is the source of my being, and it works. Then why is it that I can do everything but pray when I'm praying? I tried saying them in my head, where a lot of things get lost. I've tried saying them out loud, which only means whatever I'm saying is just louder. I've tried writing my prayers in a journal only to find my journal primarily serves as my to-do list. I tried praying in the car. Everywhere I go, I have a twenty-minute drive; but I couldn't even tell you how I got to where I was going, let alone anything about my prayer. Try as I may, my prayers are a little more like an APD (Attention Prayer Deficiency.) This is not a term you will find in a medical journal – not now, anyway.

A gift I have from God is organizing, but sometimes I feel it is a curse. On rare occasions, and I do mean rare, my brain will actually focus just on my prayers, but most of the time they go something like this:

PRAYER	WHAT I'M REALLY SAYING
Thank you for my children.	Destini has a concert tonight at 7:00. Dustin needs his tracksuit cleaned. Damon has a basketball game out of town on Friday. Homework needs to be done.
Thank you for our food.	When I get groceries I need bread, milk, eggs, cereal, hamburger meat. Hang on God, while I write this down.
Thank you for my husband.	He's working late, so I need a backup plan to get the kids where they need to go. Oh- oh, I forgot to get stuff for his lunch. Let me put that on my list.
Help the church to grow in number, knowledge, and love for you.	I need to get craft supplies for my Sunday school class, so I'll stop at the store after I get groceries. There's a potluck this Sunday. Wonder if I can pull off spaghetti again?
Thank you for all you've given us.	The car needs an oil change. I need to clean the bathrooms. Did I pick up the shower cleaner the last time I was at the store? The grass needs to be cut.
Forgive me for feeling ill toward others.	I can't believe she did that to me. Just wait until I see her again. You know, a little zap to her wouldn't hurt.
In your name, Amen	I'm out of here. Now, where's my "to do list?"

Life happens. Distractions happen. It is trying to determine if the distractions are ones we can't help or ones we make ourselves. For me, they are usually ones I make myself because I have overloaded my brain. My intentions are good, but I can miss the point of where my focus should be. I could be a Mary, or I could be a Martha, as in Luke 10:38-42.

As Jesus and his disciples continued on their way to Jerusalem, they came to a certain village where a woman named Martha welcomed him into her home. Her sister, Mary, sat at the Lord's feet, listening to what he taught. But Martha was distracted by the big dinner she was preparing. She came to Jesus and said, "Lord, doesn't it seem unfair to you that my sister just sits here while I do all the work? Tell her to help me." But the Lord said to her, "My dear Martha, you are worried and upset over all the details! There is only one thing worth being concerned about, Mary has discovered it and it will not be taken from her.

When, I am overwhelmed by the distractions, I lie in bed and just ask God to hold me. I want the distractions to stop so I can spend time with him. The words in Romans 8:26-27 are a comfort for me. For a short time, I feel his arms around me, making everything stop. I love those moments.

And the Holy Spirit helps us in our weakness. For example, we don't know what God wants us to pray. But the Holy Spirit prays for us with groaning that cannot be expressed into words. And the Father who knows all hearts knows what the Spirit is saying, for the Spirit pleads for us believers, in harmony with God's own will.

A dear friend, Nancy Combs, gave me a book, "When God Winks at You" by Squire Rushnell, which I thoroughly enjoyed reading. It is those little winks from God that reassure me he hears my prayers, no matter how I'm doing them. He hears my heartfelt prayers, my mini prayers, and my whatever you want to call them prayers. He has my back because he has my heart in his hands.

I have accepted the fact that I won't ever focus on my prayers 100% all the time, but my goal is to do it more frequently. Luckily for me, God has GAPO (God Answers Prayers Order.). Now, that should be in the medical journals.

You're Invited to a Two-Minute Pity Party

I met Lynn at church when she moved to Illinois from Texas. We had something in common. We both were mothers of small children. Her husband did not come to church with the family, but this did not stop her from bringing her children to church and being actively involved. This I admired. During one of our bible studies, Lynn said something that to this day stays with me. Her comment was that everyone is entitled to a two-minute pity party.

I liked the idea of being permitted to think anything I wanted. Here, I would tear into anyone who hurt my feelings, disagreed with me, made me feel unappreciated, or who didn't say or do what I thought they should. I could play out scenarios over and over in my head on how I would deal with certain people in my life the next time I saw them or the next time they said something. Plus, if I am only "THINKING" these thoughts and not saying them out loud, I'm not hurting anyone – so I thought.

The problem isn't that I had a two-minute pity party. The problem is that I could turn it into a "Two Week/Month/Year Pity Party." When I didn't stop at the two minutes, my thoughts consumed me. I blamed everyone and everything else, rather than taking responsibility for what I did. I drained myself physically and emotionally. Sadly, I drained myself spiritually. I didn't like the person I was becoming.

Prayer and choking down my pride helped me get back onto the right track. God answered my prayers by knocking me off my pedestal, which I made pretty high. Once I picked myself up, I could see what my purpose in life should be, and that is to serve him. My little discomfort is nothing compared to what he went through for me.

Now, don't get me wrong - I'm not there. I'm still learning to control my pity parties. I can relate oh so well with Paul with his struggle with sin in Romans 7: 18-20.

And I know that nothing good lives in me, that is, my sinful nature. I want to do what is right, but I can't. I don't want to do what is wrong, but I do it anyway. But if I do what I don't want to do, I am not really the one doing wrong. It is sin living in me that does it.

Here are the Top Ten things I do that help me stay on the right path a little longer.

1. Don't borrow trouble by dwelling on my thoughts. Thoughts can cause me to sin.
2. I must start my day with prayer, asking God to direct my thoughts and what comes out

of my mouth to be words that would glorify him. Personally, I don't know how he has time for anyone else, because controlling my thoughts and mouth is a full-time job. I'm sure he has Gabriel on speed dial for backup.

3. I'm not on Facebook, but I know I need to be careful of how I write an email or letter. Social media can increase the chance of being misunderstood, no matter how many emojis I use.

4. If someone responds to me using social media, I need to read and reread it to make sure I'm not on the defense, truly open up my heart to "hear" what the person is writing, and then wait before responding.

5. Talk face to face to the person, making myself extremely vulnerable because the walls that I put up to protect myself are gone.

6. For every negative thought I have, replace it with two positive ones.

7. I don't live in an ice-covered palace with an ice-covered staircase, I can't stand at the top of it and sing "Let it Go" like Elsa in the movie *Frozen*. I sing praise songs.

8. Be totally honest with myself by accepting the fact that I could be wrong, and I

probably did or am still doing what I find as fault in others.

9. Focus on turning my negative thoughts into something productive by getting off my high horse and physically serving someone else, especially someone I don't know that well, or that someone who consumes my thoughts.

10. Vent my thoughts personally to someone I trust. I have been blessed to have several family and friends who will be there for me. One person in particular is Kathy Meyer, who is my friend, sister in Christ and running partner. These runs are therapy sessions. While running I am venting out loud, which helps put things in perspective. I never have to ask her not to say anything to anyone. It may be that the lack of oxygen from the run causes us not to remember our conversation, or the fact we are both at the age where the memory is a - "What was I saying?"

Having a little self-pity is not a bad thing. It's the dwelling on the self-pity that pulls us farther and farther from God, and not being with Him is the biggest pity of all.

Your Mission Field, Should You Choose to Accept

The Church of Christ in Ocala, Florida, supports mission work in Barbados. Jody, a minister in Ocala along with his wife Melisa, went to Barbados several times to work with the church there. Not only did they uplift each other when they worshipped together, everyone helped spread God's word to surrounding communities.

Between these trips, Jodi and Melisa used Skype or emails as a way to encourage and reinforce God's teachings for those in Barbados. It became evident to them that this type of communication was not enough. Sadly, struggles were challenging the church in Barbados. Their next visit took them on a month-long mission.

The church in Barbados was slowly getting away from the biblical teachings of Christ. Some of the church leaders in Barbados positioned themselves to misuse their power rather than serving God.. There were conflicts within families to be faithful to each other and to God. The church needed guidance to get back to God and His teachings.

When Jody and Melisa returned to the states, Jody gave a presentation to the congregation of their mission.

Jody told of two young men at the church in Barbados in their twenties who were doing most of the preaching. He along with others who were part of this mission trip mentored them. Listening to Jody talk about this part made me reflect on a young man in the bible named, Timothy. The apostle Paul took Timothy under his wing to teach him the words of God. Now, these experienced older men were doing the same for these two young preachers.

Jody showed slides of Melisa, and other women who were part of this mission trip, working with women and their families in Barbados both physically and spiritually. They were shown by the example of these beautiful Christian women the unlimited love and value God has for those who serve him.

Jody's and Melisa's work in Barbados also reminded me of Paul's mission trips to churches he helped plant or already existed. He either wrote letters or personally visited them. Jody's and Melisa's trip encouraged me to reread the letters Paul wrote to the churches as if he were speaking to me. I thought I had a good sense of his letters, but I admit the study was deeper than I anticipated, and I realized I knew squat.

I encourage you to take a letter and read through it as though Paul were writing to you or the church where you worship. Paul's letters are ones of joy, thanksgiving, uplifting, and reprimanding. Paul stresses the importance of the churches to be united in following God. We need to be spiritually prepared.

Paul reminds us to be aware of false teachings, especially within the church. He wrote of challenges churches faced in his time, many of which churches still face today.

Through your study, you will get to know Paul and his work for God in helping the churches. There are times I find Paul is easy to understand and others times he overwhelms me. have to remember that scriptures are inspired by God, not man. The scriptures are for teaching, rebuking, and correcting. I don't know about you, but I like the teaching part, not the rebuking or correcting part.

I want the scriptures to work into my way of thinking. Yet, the bottom line is I need to take a look at God's word and accept my mission, no matter where my field takes me.

The Twelve

Twelve people with twelve distinctive personalities set out on a mission trip to the poorest part of Atlanta, Georgia. We were going to the inner city to share God's message .

Nine of us were together on a previous trip to the rural area of Pikesville, Kentucky. This was the first mission trip for the other three. Working in the inner city was going to be a new experience for all the team members.

Before we left Illinois for the 14-hour trip, everyone was given an assignment and a rough idea of the intended plan. We arrived late that night. The sponsoring organization informed us of a change in plans. Instead of a team working together, we were split up into three groups. Supplies had to be redistributed and lessons had to be replanned. While this had the makings of a disaster, we all worked well into the night to prepare for the new plan.

Each group had its own daily schedule. They worked together to complete it by being open to experiences, knowledge, and ideas from each one, no matter what the age.

They painted a stairwell in a compact area, trying to leave more paint on the wall than on themselves.

They experienced the summer bugs, heat, and humidity. They learned to ignore the "perfumed bodies" walking around since they couldn't take showers until 8:00 at night.

They had gotten used to the flattened air mattress and long car trips to the various destinations in rough traffic.

They learned they could do a prayer or devotional with little notice that started and ended the day.

They saw the importance of the mission rules to go out two by two, as there were some intense situations with the homeless while bringing food and conversation to them.

Their hearts broke when they saw children in those food lines.

They tried desperately to spread themselves to each child seeking attention, while conducting Vacation Bible School in the housing projects.

They felt their hearts filling with compassion for those they visited in the nursing home.

They saw each positive situation and each negative situation molding their hearts into one.

They understood a little more the words spoken by Martin Luther King Jr. "I have a dream," when they walked where he walked.

Twelve people with twelve personalities came back from a trip from the poorest part of Atlanta to find they were richer in respect, understanding, acceptance, and love for not only those they served, but for each other.

David, David, David

For months it seemed like every Bible study, preaching, devotionals I read, or even when worshipping with other churches while vacationing, all had to do with David. I have to admit I was getting a little tired of hearing about David. After all, there were other people in the Bible, especially some great women. I couldn't help thinking about a scene in the television show, The Brady Bunch, when Jan Brady was feeling left out because the world seemed to revolve around her older sister, Marsha. Her famous words from that scene were, "Marsha, Marsha, Marsha." Now, I found myself thinking, "David, David, David."

Scripture tells us David was a man after God's own heart. He fills the book of Psalms with his beautiful words about his life with God as though it was his own diary. So why was I getting tired of hearing about David and feeling bad for thinking this way? Perhaps I felt I didn't have anything in common with him. I wasn't a shepherd boy. I didn't play the harp. I didn't kill a giant. I didn't command an army. I didn't run a kingdom. I didn't commit adultery. I didn't have a man killed. I didn't have people wanting to kill me. I didn't have a prophet to personally talk to for advice. Then one day while doing my devotional, I came across Psalm 39:1-3.

I said, I will watch my ways and keep my tongue from sin; I will put a muzzle on my mouth while in the presence of the wicked. I remained utterly silent, not even saying anything good. But my anguish increased; my heart grew hot within me. While I meditated, the fire burned; then I spoke with my tongue.

Yes, David and I did have something in common! We let things fester inside us. The first chance we got we were going to let those who offend us experience our righteous wrath.

But, reading further, I realized I was taking things out of context. God wasn't using David to tell us it is okay to go off on people. Rather, David took the turmoil that was growing in his thought straight to God. He did not want the turmoil to grow in his heart - bummer. He asked God to remind him of his place, for his only hope for everything he is going through while here on earth is in the Lord.

Through the scriptures we can see the up close and personal life of David and how God uses his life to preserve the lineage of Jesus. God gave us David so that everyone could relate to him on some level. We may see it right away, or we may have to dwell in his word a little more to see what we have in common. We will have something in common.

If truth be told, I guess David and I have more in common than I'd like to admit - pride, arrogance, bossing people around. You know the "little sins." Also, while writing this I realized that David and I may have something else in common. We both are writers. Although my words may not be as poetic as David's, I pray they are words that God wants written. Words that He guides from my heart, not my head, in hopes of bringing us all to someone we do have in common..."God, God, God."

The Transport

We were returning to Illinois from a trip to Florida. As I was driving on I-57, I noticed lights flashing in the distance behind me. I and others pulled over to the side of the road to give this vehicle safe passage. It seemed like forever until the emergency vehicle was beside us. As it passed, I saw "PEDIATRIC TRANSPORT" written on its side. My heart sank, and tears came to me at the thought of a child being inside. I never saw a transport vehicle like this, and could only imagine what everyone was going through. I prayed that God would protect the child, driver, parents, and those taking care of this child.

Once the flashing lights were out of sight, I couldn't help thinking that we are like this vehicle in that our bodies transport our souls. If others saw a sign on us that said, "SOUL TRANSPORT" would their hearts sink? Would tears come to them? Would they pray? Would they clear the way for us?

Just like the driver of that emergency vehicle was on a mission to get the child to the destination, we too should do the same for our journey. We must have our sirens blaring and lights flashing so others can see that our bodies are transporting a soul.

Online Order

Recently I did my first online grocery order through Walmart. I put it off for a long time. I thought it would take too much time to search for the food I wanted and then double check my order. I also hesitated to give them my financial information.

On that day, as I was writing a list of ingredients I needed for a dish I was bringing to a party, I thought, "Why do this twice?" So, I went to the website.

I found it easy to do, and clicking "submit" not to be as hard as I thought. In fact, I was anticipating picking up my order. When that time came, everything was ready as promised. The person delivering my order was extremely helpful and polite. I definitely will do this again.

On the way home I got to thinking, wouldn't it be great if I could order my Christianity the same way? For instance, I could order a pound of kindness, a gallon of forgiveness, a carton of empathy, a bag of memorized scriptures, a dozen acts of serving.

I could order wipes that would clean up any negative words that came out of my mouth, softeners for my heart, and vitamins that would prevent any sin before spreading. But, the most amazing thing about ordering my Christianity online is that I would never have to submit any financial information for the total cost would say, "Paid in full."

On or Off

It is winter in Bonfield, Illinois, where the sunlight is limited this time of the year. But one Sunday morning, while sitting in church, I noticed the sun was shining through the windows. The brightness and warmth of the sunshine definitely makes me stop to thank our Creator.

The singing that morning was warming my soul. Some people were singing the melody, some harmony, some on key, and some off-key. It was wonderful! But, what I loved more was seeing people smiling at each other as we were worshipping God.

John and I have been blessed to be able to travel a little more the last few years. This has given us the opportunity to visit other churches. Every church had its unique outreach program. Some stood out to us more than others, especially when we felt we were part of the church family.

This particular Sunday, I reflected on those previous travels. I remembered how I felt when visiting various churches. Why did some stick with me more than others? It occurred to me that I felt the most welcomed when the sun was shining through the church windows. There was light. The auditorium wasn't dark, and there was no spotlight on those in front. When a spotlight is on,

I tend to focus my attention to the lighted area. I have to remind myself to worship with the whole church. Sometimes I have to work on staying awake. My drooling while snoring is not a pretty sight.

I feel more of God's presence when there is light. I love being outside enjoying the nature God created. A scene in "Soul Surfer" showed a church service on the beach. Can you imagine singing praise to God on a beach overlooking the ocean? John and I never had the opportunity to do this. We got close when we helped chaperon a youth group to Turkey Run State Park in Indiana. We hiked until we found some beautiful rocks off the trail where we all could sit. This is where we worshipped God. It was amazing.

While visiting other churches I saw more worship centers, auditoriums, sanctuaries, or whatever they may be called, with no windows. I'm sure there is a reason for this. Could it be so people don't feel like they are in church or some kind of organized religion? Is it done so as not to draw attention to those who do fall asleep? Could the leadership be trying to orchestrate the worship in a way that guides or even controls our feelings? Maybe this is the modern version of what was done years ago by singing ten verses to "Just As I Am," while the minister is waving his bible over his head. He just knows there is someone in the congregation that needs to come forward to repent.

Of course, having lights on or off, or having or not having windows is not a salvation issue. You will not find a book, chapter, or verse concerning this subject in the Bible or any thoughts in a commentary. As I wrote earlier, I love the outdoors. You may prefer to be indoors and enjoy the darkness when it comes to worshipping. Neither one is wrong.

Funny how God gives you little nudges when you're deep in thought with him. For some reason, I was reminded of a radio commercial about a motel. It ended with these words. "I'm Tom Bodett for Motel 6, and we'll leave the light on for you."

If you worship with a church that turns the lights off, I encourage you to leave them on. Who knows, you may be pleasantly surprised by whom you see.

OK, God

We live in a time where we want everything yesterday. Now, before you roll your eyes or nod in agreement because you think I'm talking just about the younger generations, know that you could be wrong. No matter the generation, we all at some time in our life don't want to wait on anyone or anything. This includes electronic devices that we think we just can't live without that are used and misused across ALL generations. These devices can forecast the weather, tell a joke, correct spelling, raise or lower toilet seats, turn lights on or off, lock or unlock doors, set timers, text or call someone, set reminders, recite trivia questions, give us directions, select our favorite music, or find a virtual friend. All we have to do is say, "OK Google," or "Alexa," or "Cortana, or Siri."

I'm just starting to use my Google Assistant more on my Android phone. I wondered how it answers Bible questions. My first question was, "OK Google, What does the Bible say about marriage?" It went right to a scripture, and even read it for me. I was impressed!

I then ventured on asking questions about what the Bible says about sexuality, baptism, communion, giving, worshipping, church divisions - you know the general questions for which we all want the Bible to agree with our viewpoint. I'm not sure if I was only allowed one direct Bible quote or if I was wearing out my Assistant by asking questions. After my one "freebie," Google Assistant replied saying, "I can search the web for you." Perhaps my Google Assistant wanted to be politically correct by staying on the fence when faced with questions that could be controversial. When reading the information given to me by my Google Assistant, I read scriptures as well as various religious and non-religious viewpoints. If I didn't like what one person said, I could easily find someone to agree with me.

While these devices can be fun and helpful, I challenge all of us to use another source for our religious questions. The Bible, the book. Not the electronic version. Let's use our hands to touch the pages of the Bible to look up scripture. Let's use paper and pen to make our own notes or better yet underline and highlight scripture. Let's use book resources such as commentaries, Bible dictionaries, concordance, maps, etc. I do have to confess since I'm using my laptop to write this, it is easier to click on a web search for a certain topic or look up a verse than to get up and get my Bible. It's a work in progress, but there is something about that open Bible.

Once you have your research tools ready, begin by saying: "Ok, God, open my heart to read your words, rather than defend my views." But, here's a warning.- chances are really good that we are not going to like everything we read because God isn't politically correct, he is God correct. Yet, if we are really quiet and have our hearts truly open, we just might hear, "OK, my child. Let's begin."

Lessons from Solomon

Did you ever have one of those days when you felt like the best Christian in the world? On rare occasions, I do. My halo is so straight and bright that all those around me are in awe. I want to volunteer to teach a Bible class, help with Vacation Bible School, outreach ministries, or any kind of mission work. I can do something for anyone, never asking questions or giving my opinion on how they should do things. Unfortunately, it is usually short-lived, but it could be longer if people wouldn't get in my way.

A while back, I experienced being extremely negative, judgmental, and opinionated. I justified my feelings in a way that convinced others to agree with me. This way I could save face and not be held accountable for any consequences. Yet, I didn't like how I was feeling. Even if it was rough, I needed people to help me become accountable.

It seemed that no matter where I started with my Bible study or heard thoughts by others, I was being directed to the book of Proverbs. I decided this was God's way of saying, "Hello Melinda, just a little reminder that you are not God." So starting with the book of Proverbs, it was. Even though I had read it many times before, it was like I was experiencing it for the first time. Proverbs opens with the reason for the writing of this book.

Proverbs 1: 1-7

1. These are the proverbs of Solomon, David's son, king of Israel.

2. Their purpose is to teach people wisdom and discipline, to help them understand the insights of the wise.

3. Their purpose is to teach people to live disciplined and successful lives, to help them do what is right, just, and fair.

4. These proverbs will give insight to the simple, knowledge and discernment to the young.

5. Let the wise listen to these proverbs and become even wiser. Let those with understanding receive guidance

6. by exploring the meaning in these proverbs and parables, the words of the wise and their riddles.

7. Fear of the LORD is the foundation of true knowledge, but fools despise wisdom and discipline.

I knew if I wanted to stop being negative, judgmental, or opinionated, I needed to learn from some of the best teachers in the world - my children, who at times are as wise as Solomon.

Lesson One

When a child sees someone needing money, they will just give it and want nothing in return.

When our children were little, we were on a family trip. We were getting off the interstate when our daughter, Destini, saw a homeless man holding a sign saying he needed money. As John and I were looking for the locks on our door, Destini rolled down her window to give the man her change. I was about to tell her of the dangers of doing this, but stopped when I saw tears in her eyes for the man. Destini knew what it was to give unconditionally.

I would think or say something like, "They could get a job if they really wanted. It's probably beneath them to work at a fast-food restaurant. This begging is their job."

Those who oppress the poor insult their Maker, But helping the poor honors Him. - Proverbs 14:31

Lesson Two

When a child sees someone needing help, he just does it. They don't ask what's in it for me.

When our son, Damon's first-grade teacher called, I instantly thought, "Oh no - a call from the teacher is not good." However, she wanted to share with us that there was a child in the class that was being teased by some children, and no one wanted to play with him. Damon had taken it upon himself to take this child under his wing to protect him and play with him. She said this was something she had only seen one other time in all her years of teaching. Damon knew what it was to care for someone unconditionally.

I would think or say something like, "Well, if they are in this predicament, it is because they don't know how to do anything on their own. If they want to better themselves, they should do this or that. I will help them, but only for a few hours. After all, this is my day off and I have things I need to do for myself."

Fools have no interest in understanding; they only want to air their own opinions. - Proverbs 18:2

Lesson Three

When a child is in Bible class, he is the first to raise his hand to lead a song, pray, or answer questions about the story.

When our son, Dustin, was stationed at Camp LeJeune, he was asked to teach a children's Bible class. Instead of giving excuses, he took it upon himself to study the material and observe others. This led him to teaching classes not only for children but to adults, leading songs, and even preaching - be it in the United States, Okinawa, Afghanistan, or Iraq. Dustin knew what it was to serve unconditionally.

I would say or think something like, "I don't know how. I'm not good with that age. I am retired. I'm busy. Get someone else to do it. I've done my part. I don't want to give up going to my class."

Commit your work to the Lord, and then your plans will succeed. Proverbs 16:3

Being a Christian doesn't mean we should let people walk over us like a worn-out doormat. This doesn't help anyone. But, if we truly want to serve God, our hearts must become a welcoming mat, so all can see his unconditional love.

Nothing New Under the Sun

I am not on Facebook. I know there is some good on it, like the family pictures, but it is something I choose not to do. My husband showed me a posting from his Facebook page. After reading it I got upset and yelled, "Seriously, I can't believe that person wrote that!" and "This is why I'm not on Facebook!" He finally learned to screen what he shows me. Now he shows me dishes that I can make with just a snap of my finger or the waving of my hand.

Even with that said, one day he pointed out something he thought I would find interesting to read. I found out later, it was posted by my beautiful, talented, and tender-hearted granddaughter, Belinda, which I say without any bias. It was an article entitled, "59 Percent of Millennials Raised in a Church Have Dropped Out – And They're Trying to Tell Us Why" by Sam Eaton.

John was right, I did find it interesting and took what Sam had written to heart. He put a lot of thought, heart, and soul into writing this article. Not only did he give his own twelve reasons as to why the Millennials are dropping out of church, he also gave solutions for these issues.

While reading his article, I must admit I laughed a little to myself as I was reminded of Solomon's saying, *Nothing new under the sun.* Sam's article is well written, but his thoughts have been voiced, discussed to death, prayed about, moved on from, caused divisions by so many other people, since the beginning of man - be it church or society in general. Is God not the first to be upset with the generations of men He Himself made?

Sam's writings took me back to my generation hearing our elders say, "In my generation blah, blah, blah. I could remember being upset at hearing this and vowing I would never say that. Well... that came back to bite me along with, "When I was your age," and "In my day." It was a good thing I didn't have to ride a horse or walk to school while carrying my shoes.

As I did more research after reading Sam's article, I came across one written by Dr. Jill Novak, University of Phoenix, Texas A&M University, entitled, "The Six Living Generations in America." She gave detailed descriptions of each generation, which are:

- ➢ GI Generation (born 1901-1926)
- ➢ Mature/Silents 1927-1945)
- ➢ Baby boomer (1946-1964)
- ➢ Generation X (1965-1980)
- ➢ Millennial/Generation Y 1981-2000)
- ➢ Generation Z 2000 – 2012)

I couldn't help laughing, because again there was nothing new under the sun. No matter what generation you fall in, there are some people in every generation who blame the previous or the current generation for the troubles in the church.

A couple of days after reading these articles, John and I were watching "Last Man Standing." We have always enjoyed the subtle comments referring to God on the show, which always made us laugh. The episode that night devoted a large portion to religion/God, where Mike and Vanessa Baxter were concerned about two of their daughters not going to church.

Mike was convinced it was from the boring sermons. He took it upon himself to help the minister spice things up to keep everyone interested. The following Sunday, the minister had people "glued to the pew" with laughter. Mike felt good in his accomplishments and just knew his daughters would want to come back. Although they enjoyed the sermon, they had no intention of returning.

He finally figured out church wasn't about entertainment, although his idea to help the minister was a big help. His involvement is what was truly needed. From there, using his dad's charm, he guided his daughters to use their talents for the church.

How wonderful it would be if someone, no matter what generation, could solve the ongoing problem of how to keep people from dropping out of church. Who knows, maybe by then I'll be on Facebook.

Friendly Begins with Me

In September of 2017, John and I took a trip to South Dakota. On Sunday morning we worshipped in a Church of Christ in the town of Custer. We were a few minutes late to Bible class due to buffalo crossing the road. They might have moved a little faster if thy heard John's rendition of Roger Miller's "You Can't Roller Skate in a Buffalo Herd."

When Bible class was over, two men introduced themselves to us. Shortly after talking with them, I realized they were visitors. They didn't know if we were regulars or visitors, but that didn't matter. They just started a conversation. I commented to one of them that I was impressed that he did this. I shared with him that there were churches we visited who may have implied a "hi" with quick eye contact or a nod of their head as they walked past us on their way to the door. This led to further discussion that sadly some churches don't know the regular attendees from visitors. We shared the same insight as to why, and both agreed that knowing people takes commitment. And since we all are the church, we must do this no matter where we are worshipping. He then said something that has stayed with me since that day: "No matter where I am, or if someone does or does not take the time to make me feel part of the church, friendly begins with me."

I am fairly sure this church that morning would probably know who the visitors were, as their normal attendance is around twelve. However, that day there were around 40. You could feel the excitement of us all being together for worship.

Even with the small number, there were still those who implied a "hi" with quick eye contact or a nod of their head as they passed us on their way to the door. However, many stayed after worship to talk. There were no visitors, no regulars, no conservatives, no liberals, no traditional, no non-traditional, only plain old Christians – the church – the body of Christ who came together because of one person who lived what he believed.

"Friendly begins with me."

Finding the One

Luke 15:1-4

Tax collectors and other notorious sinners often came to listen to Jesus teach.

This made the Pharisees and teachers of religious law complain that he was associating with such sinful people—even eating with them!

So Jesus told them this story:

If a man has a hundred sheep and one of them gets lost, what will he do? Won't he leave the ninety-nine others in the wilderness and go to search for the one that is lost until he finds it?

Jesus used this parable in hopes of reaching the Pharisees and teachers of the law to show that his teachings were for everyone. Not just for the select few.

The shepherd, in this parable, with 100 sheep was probably considered wealthy. But when the one was lost he didn't say, "I have 99 more, so losing one is no big deal." Rather, he knew this one sheep was in danger, and he needed to find that sheep. He would have done the same for any of his sheep who were under his care.

99

I think I'm a good shepherd - doing whatever is needed to find the lost one. I find at time, I'm only a good shepherd when it's convenient

It is easy to reach out to those at church who are in my "home flock." There are some who may not feel like they are part of the flock, not come all the time, and then wander off for various reasons.

I must ask myself, "Do I stay with the flock or do I go after the one that is lost?" It's easy for me to rationalize my thoughts to not go after the one by saying:

> "How do they expect to get anything out of church when they come occasionally, only one hour a week, or come late and leave early?"
> "Why do they feel left out of things? After all, information about church happenings is announced in the bulletin, posted on the bulletin board, posted on Facebook, the church website, or sent out in a church text."
> "If they or someone in their family feels left out, why don't they go to the person(s) in charge and let it be known? Better yet, do something to make sure others don't feel the same way they do."

- ➤ "Are they upset because no one calls them when they aren't at church, sick, or in the hospital? How many people did they call or visit?"

- ➤ "If they have hurt feelings toward someone, do they wait for others to make the first move? When neither makes a move, do they let themselves off the hook by saying, "I forgive ___" without ever having a face-to-face, heart-to-heart conversation?

- ➤ "Why do they rave about going to programs, concerts, or events at other churches and then comment on how we could do these events, but do nothing to organize them?"

- ➤ "When something new is introduced to help the church grow, are they the first to complain or do they encourage others to embrace the change?"

- ➤ "Socials with physical food is a great way to fellowship . Why do they not see the importance of coming to church to find the spiritual food that brings us together so we can stay strong in our faith?"

- ➤ "Why do they not see the importance, the blessing, and the privilege of sharing the communion to remember what Christ did for us?"

I could go on and on in my self-righteousness as my halo sits firmly on my head, assuming I'm right. Sadly, I too am the lost one. Some days I can do, say, and think what God wants, and then there are other days I don't want to be a grownup. I want to be the one that leaves others, hoping no one comes looking for me. I don't want to be responsible or accountable to anyone – especially to God. I know this isn't what he expects from me. This kind of thinking, talking, and action is cheap. It builds up no one. It slowly tears down the church.

I cannot take the easy way out by not going after the one that is lost. I need to get off my high horse (you might think by now I have learned the fall doesn't get any easier) and actually do something like:

> - Personally telling them they are missed at church.
> - Personally offering any help to get them to church or activities.
> - Personally inviting them to church happenings. Just don't assume they know about them.
> - Praying with them, for them, not at them.
> - Stop judging – even if it is in a "Christian" way.

- ➢ Validating their concerns for the church and devise a plan addressing them.
- ➢ Together, reaffirming what we as a church need to do to serve God.
- ➢ Offering to do a one on one Bible study – even if I don't know all the answers.
- ➢ Offering to teach or sub for a class.
- ➢ Offering to oversee a program or help those who are overseeing a program.
- ➢ Working hard on making people feel welcome, be they age 3 or 103.
- ➢ Helping them see the importance of the body of Christ – His church.
- ➢ Stop justifying feelings, and going to the person that I may have issues with and asking them to forgive me.
- ➢ Not getting discouraged when ideas are met with opposition, and praying that the ideas are ones that glorify God.

In other words, swallowing my pride, opening my heart, coming out of my comfort zone, stopping complaining, stopping assuming someone else will do it, so not to give Satan any more hold on the church.

Luke 15:5-7

And when he has found it, he will joyfully carry it home on his shoulders.

When he arrives, he will call together his friends and neighbors, saying, 'Rejoice with me because I have found my lost sheep.'

In the same way, there is more joy in heaven over one lost sinner who repents and returns to God than over ninety-nine others who are righteous and haven't strayed away!

Excuses

I try to be a good Christian. I could be more of one, if life didn't get in the way. My goal is to spend comparable time reading my bible, praying, reaching out to others, going to church, as I do in working out, taking care of the family, visiting with friends, or going to work.

There are examples of amazing people in the Bible who have accomplished this. Jesus was a carpenter, Paul a tentmaker, the worthy woman in Proverbs ran a business while taking care of her family, and Lydia was a seller of purple cloth. They never gave God excuses for why he could not be first. Being the human I am, with my tilting halo, when life gets in the way God is placed way down on my list of priorities. He's the one who hears excuse after excuse of why he can't be first.

Excuses to God:

1. The time church starts isn't convenient for me. Sunday is the only day I can sleep in.
2. It's too cold, hot, dark, sunny, foggy, windy, rainy, snowy for me to get out of the house.
3. I don't get anything out of the classes, sermons, or singing.
4. I don't like the attitude of some of the people.

5. If I come I'm expected to get involved. No one listens to my ideas, so why bother?

If I gave my children the same excuses I give God, Family Services could be called.

1. The time you all get up isn't convenient for me. I'd like to sleep in too.
2. It's too cold, hot, dark, sunny, foggy, windy, rainy, snowy for us to go outside to play.
3. I don't get anything out of cleaning the house, you all just mess it up again.
4. I don't get anything out of cooking, no one wants the same thing and it's never ending. I don't know why you think you must eat three times a day.
5. You all are wanting me to do something like change your diapers, go to your games, recitals. It never ends.
6. No one listens to me. You do whatever you want to do.

If I gave my employer the same excuses I give God, I could be fired.

1. The time you want me to be at work isn't convenient for me. I need my eight hours of sleep.

2. It's too cold, hot, dark, sunny, foggy, windy, rainy, snowy for me to get out of the house to go to work.
3. I don't get anything out of work. Everyone complains, and it's the same thing over and over.
4. You expect me to come to work before I go on vacations, have fun with my friends, scheduling appointments. Why can't you work around me?
5. I don't like the attitudes of some of the people.
6. If I start doing work related things for you, then you'll expect me to do it all the time. I might consider doing something if I get a raise, or more employee benefits.
7. You don't value my input. Management does what it wants to do.

Many of us probably wouldn't give these excuses to our family or employer. Sadly, we do at times give them to God. Luckily for us all, God wants us to be with him and never gives excuses.

II Peter 3:9

The Lord is not slow in keeping his promise, as some understand slowness. Instead he is patient with you, not wanting anyone to perish, but everyone to come to repentance.

What's That Smell?

I attended Jed Yancey's Sunday school class in September of 2018 at the Central Church of Christ in Ocala, Florida. He is a young man with an old soul. He shared his experiences from his childhood, his profession, love of sports, and open-ended questions to help us relate to the lesson.

On this Sunday, Jed asked us if we remembered ever stepping in dog poop, and what we used to remove the poop. Most answered a small stick.

When asked this question, I instantly thought of the time I went for a run while visiting our son Dustin and his family at Camp LeJeune, North Carolina. He directed me to a path close to their house. My daughter-in-law, Maki, told me to watch out for the dog poop because no one took the time to clean up after their dogs. I heeded her words of caution and forged onto the path.

Do we ever hear the word of God but forge onto the wrong path anyway?

I was running along, enjoying the sunshine and the scenery. I didn't take the time to look for dog poop. Occasionally, I looked around on the ground. Not seeing anything, I assumed people did take the time to pick up after their dogs.

Do we trick ourselves to thinking, "How can this be sin when I'm enjoying my life from God?"

Yet, when I got home and started to take off my shoes, the smell was so raunchy it took my breath. Both shoes were covered in thick dog poop from toe to heel and going up the sides toward the inside of my shoes. I didn't know how I was going to get them off without touching some of the poop. There was no using a small stick or a stick of any size. I honestly thought the only thing I could do was carefully put them in a bag and throw them away.

Do we ever feel the sin in our lives is so deep that God will only want to throw us away?

I really didn't want to throw the shoes away, because they weren't that old and running shoes aren't cheap. So I held my breath, pulled as quickly as I could, and took them over to the hose. I was holding the nozzle as close to the shoes as I could, spraying at full blast and trying not to get poop on me. This did not work, and now poop was on me as well.

Do we ever forget what Christ did for us to wash away our sins?

After I got them "hand cleaned," they went into the washer on the hottest water and sanitizer available. I headed for the shower, doing the same.

We both came out sparkling clean with no lingering smell.

I still have those shoes, and when I go out for a run they remind me of how God guides me. He won't give up on me, and He will never ask, "What's that smell?"

The Sweetest Sound Ever

There are so many sounds I love to hear - the chirping of birds out my window before rising for the day, the waves crashing onto the shore, and laughter at family gatherings. But for me, the sweetest sound ever is that of children, especially in church.

I love to hear babies cooing, giggling, and even crying. I love hearing toddlers who think they are whispering when asking questions, laughing, singing, or even occasionally being a little "expressive." Of course, this is easy for me to say as it's been forty years since I tried to keep a little one quiet in church.

One Sunday morning Jax, who is preschool age, ran to the front of the church and down the middle aisle, which is something he had never done before. He brought smiles to many of us. I was talking with his mother after church, and she shared a wonderful story of why he was running. He knew that after the big people ate dinner (aka communion) he got to go to Sunday School (aka Children's Church) which he so enjoyed. However, this particular morning there were some people blocking his normal path, so he turned and ran in a different direction to get to Children's Church. What a wonderful lesson for all of us. He wanted to be at Children's Church. He saw an obstacle. Instead of giving up, he ran in the other direction to get to his destination. How many of us desire this when we go to church?

When I was a young mother, I was blessed by older women in the church who kept reassuring me that I was a good mother. They helped me by not judging me. Rather, they lifted me up when I experienced self-doubt. Sometimes I didn't like their advice, but all conversations ended in prayer for me.

Their love and words of encouragement are things I want to share with all young parents who may feel a little overwhelmed bringing their children to church.

First, you are doing the most important work as a parent, sharing God with your child. Yes, you will need to discipline your child on occasion while at church, which you would expect to do when taking them to restaurants, school, special occasions, etc. There were some occasions when I had to take our oldest son Damon out of church when he was "expressing himself." No matter how smoothly I thought I was doing this, he would grab several chairs on the way, creating a scene. I guess turnaround was fair play, as I can remember my mother taking me out and my not going willfully, since I knew I would not get a talking-to, but rather a hand on my bottom.

Second, by being in church consistently, even if you never hear a song, sermon, or just want to run out when the last amen is said, you are telling your children God is first in your lives. Being consistent when they are young is so important. It will be your salvation should they spread their wings as teenagers.

Third, the sound of babies, toddlers, and young children is the sound of a church growing. You are teaching them what it means to be part of the family of God. You are teaching them about a serving heart, which helps them strive to become a teacher, deacon, elder, minister, missionary, or wherever God directs them.

Young families are in my prayers that they will remain strong for God, and for them letting me hear the sweetest sound ever - .their children.

A Chance Meeting

When asked to speak at Ladies Days at different churches I always included a story, as I felt stories were a way of getting your point across without being "preachy." A storyteller knows their audience within the first few minutes. You know whether the story you chose will work or if you have to change it in a split second. I prepared this story, but not as my first choice. It involved dialogue between two people. The last time I did a duo dialogue I was in high school standing before my peers and judges at a County Speech Contest.

This day I was rolling in both roles. Then near the end I went completely blank. I could not finish! All I could do was sit down. However, on this particular Ladies Day at Church of Christ in South Holland, Indiana, I knew this story could be told in its entirety. Here it is.

Two women smiled at each other as they sat in the only two chairs left in the doctor's office. Both women looked as though they would give birth at any moment. One looked prepared. One looked lost. Unbeknown to each other, their children would meet.

"Hi there. I'm Joey. What's your name?"

"Tara."

"That's a nice name. How do ya like the doctor?"

"He's O.K."

"Yeah, but man when he puts that stethoscope on my mom's belly it is so cold that I want to yell back, 'HEY METAL EARS, MOVE IT!' Your mom is pretty. How old is she?"

"Sixteen."

"Sixteen! Wow, she sure is a lot younger than my mom. She's twenty-two. I just hope she doesn't keel over before popping me out. I already have this vision of her being the only mom in a wheelchair pushing me on the swings. When are you going to be born?"

"Any time."

"Any time! Me too. Maybe we'll see each other at the hospital. You sure are little to be born anytime soon."

"I know. My mom has a rough time with me inside of her and she has to take some pills, and get some shots, and drink some stuff to make her feel better. I get to sleep a lot, that way I don't bother her or make her mad when I move around. Does your mom take the same kind of medicine?"

"I don't think so. My mom doesn't get mad when I move. She gets so excited, but not as bad as my dad. He goes crazy. He puts things on my mom's belly to see how far I can kick them. He actually puts marks on the wall. That's him sitting next to my mom. I hope he doesn't do anything embarrassing. Oh no, he's hugging us again. I'm going to be bruised from head to toe before I'm even born. Yo, dad I can't breathe. Come on, give me a break. OK, you asked for it. Hiyah! Sorry mom, but a man's gotta do what a man's gotta do. Is that your dad over there?"

"No, he doesn't come around anymore. He used to once in a while. I didn't like when he did. He yelled about money, and some pills, and then he would knock us down and it really hurt."

"That's pretty rough stuff. My dad doesn't hurt us. He gives us the neatest belly rubs. I just love them, especially when he goes around and around and around. I hate it when he goes up and down like what he is doing now. Yo, dad ya better stop it now before your finger goes up my nose. Dad move your finger. OK, you asked for it. Hiyah! Sorry mom, but I can breathe much better now, and I don't sound so nasal."

"My mom reads all the time. What about your mom?"

"Oh yes, it's a book with people that have beautiful houses, clothes, and cars. They are always going to fancy dinner parties. Me and my mom are going to live in a place like that one day. We are going to have a barn full of horses. We love horses. We're going to have hundreds of them. I'll have my own teacher who'll show me how to ride and I'll be famous all over the world. My mom takes me to the horse stables every day and tells me all about them."

"That sure sounds like a lot of fun. The only thing I know about horses is you put a quarter in them, and they play music. Maybe I can come see you someday.

My mom reads a book called the Bible. Do you know what that is?"

"No."

"Well, it's this book that tells you all sorts of neat things and how much this guy called Jesus loves us. You see His father, God, made this whole wide world and everything in it. He was proud of everything he had made, but He was sad because people were mean. Now God wanted to let everyone know how much he loved them, so he did something really special. I really don't understand it all, but He sent his son named Jesus who died on the cross for us. When mom tells me about it she usually cries and says how lucky we are to have someone love us and that she is going to love me just as much."

"Then mom gets on her knees to pray, that means she's talking to God. He doesn't talk back, but He listens real good, and has a way of answering my mom's prayers. I get scrunched up when she prays, but it's a good scrunch. I don't even kick her. Sometimes she cries when she prays. You see my daddy used to get drunk all the time; but ever since he and my mom started reading the

Bible and going to church, things have really changed. Ya know Tara, I think you would like this God guy. Maybe he could stop your dad from hitting your mom."

"Joey, he sounds great! It would be nice not to be hit all the time, but I wasn't real honest with you. My mom doesn't take medicine to feel better. We're junkies and the drugs make her feel better. I don't think this God guy would like us."

"Sure He would. That's what's really neat about Him. He wants to be a part of everyone's life and help them. Have you ever been to church?"

"No. What's a church?"

"Well it's this place where we go, and everyone is learning about how we need to do what God wants us to do. Not only do we study, but we sing and pray. Everyone there is so nice. They are always hugging mom and me and patting her belly. Now there is one lady there who has to rub my mom's belly and does she ever have bad breath! Maybe your mom will bring you there someday. It's right down the road. Trust me, you'll love it. Well, Nurse Sunshine called our name, so I guess we'll be going. I really hope to see you soon, Tara."

"Me too, Joey. I can't wait to tell my mom about this God. You know Joey, I almost feel happy."

The nurse called both ladies in at the same time. They proceed to their assigned examination room. After being reassured all was good, they returned home to await the birth. Joey's mother is the first to start her labor.

"Hey mom, I think it's time for us to boogie on down to the hospital. I think the water bed in here has a leak in it. We'd better wake up Sleeping Beauty."

"Oh no, dad ran out to the car and forgot us. Yo, dad we're still here. Somehow I don't think they'll believe you're having a baby even with all those love handles. Hey mom, I think he figured out we weren't in the car and looks like he's coming back for us. Dad, you don't need to pull mom's hand so hard. We can't walk that fast. If you just remain real cool, everything will be alright and that includes your driving. Dad watch out for that curb! Correct me if I'm wrong, but doesn't red mean stop? And doesn't a flashing red light mean police? I'm so embarrassed! While all the other babies in the nursery are wearing pink or blue I'll be wearing black and white stripes with little numbers on it. Whoa, what's happening? A police escort! Way to go, dad."

"There's the doctor. Glad to see you could make it. I sure hope he got up on the right side of the bed. After all, I'm having that little cut later and I certainly wouldn't want you to be upset about anything. Oh, oh, there's the third grunt. I'd better get moving before mom develops a hernia. Only I'm not really sure if I want to go out there. It's really nice and warm in here. Right now I really don't have to do anything. I get all the food I want and can sleep whenever I want. Things out there look pretty scary. Maybe I'll just stay here or not... that grunt sounds like you mean business. OK, a one and a two and a...

"Ta da. Mom, everyone here only has eyes. They don't have any mouths or noses. They don't look like us. They must be from outer space. Oh, wait a minute I remember now from watching all those medical shows they are wearing masks. I can't wait to see all those people at church. I bet their hugs are going to feel even greater now that they can touch me. Is it O.K. if we bring some mouthwash for that one lady? Oh, this blanket is so nice and warm. Mom stop crying and kissing all over me. It's really embarrassing. Dad, you look a little strange. A little green. Why are you on the floor? Hey God, you did alright picking my parents, but don't go too far away. We've some work cut out for us with dad. Mom, they said I'm going to the nursery now, so I catch ya later. I'm a little tired. Gonna catch some ZZZZs."

"Hey, it's awfully noisy in here. Wonder if I can get anything that's a little more private and has a view? What is that smell: Clean up in bassinet #9. Hey Tara, are you here?"

Later that night Tara's mother feels the start of her labor.

"Mommy, I can't wait to tell you about my new friend Joey and about this really neat guy he knows called God. This God sounds too good to be true. Joey says he wouldn't turn his back on us even though we're junkies. He wants to help stop our hurt. He wants to love us. Oh, mommy doesn't that sound great to have someone to love us?"

Oh, oh, Mommy, I think it's time for us to go to the hospital! Wake up. Oh, I can't wait to feel your arms around me holding me. We're going to do just fine. We'd better get going real soon. I'm so excited! Mommy, where are you going? The suitcase isn't in the bathroom. What are you doing? That needle was in the garbage. If you have to use it please get a clean one or, better yet, just put it down and let's go to the hospital. I won't move around very much. I promise. I'll be good. It's O.K. mommy we can make it. Please don't do it! If you do this I'll die, and I want to live."

"Mommy, there's some strange stuff coming close to me. Please, mommy get it out of here. Make it stop! Make it stop! I hate you! I'm sorry, I didn't mean to say that. It's so dark in here. I'm so cold. Mommy...mommy...mom...mee..."

> Hush a bye don't you cry
> Go to sleepy little baby
> When you wake you shall find
> All the pretty little horsies

Section Four - Family

Many of my stories, poems, or songs were inspired by my family - be they short and sweet, heart wrenching, or soul searching.

Anniversary Song for John

When I was just a little girl
I dreamed of my wedding day.
Colors of flowers, gown of white
And of the love I'd give away.

One thing that my husband must have
If our life should be,
A love for the Lord, a love so strong,
One deeper than for me.

It was on that summer night
A chance for us to meet
We talked of our lives, we talked of our dreams,
As our hearts found a beat.

A carpenter you wanted to be,
Which would be put on hold.
For the Army you did join
And you left scared but bold.

That coming Fall I'd go to school,
A teacher I would be.
We talked of our lives, we talked of our dreams
And changing us to we.

A wedding there would be in June
And we held each other's hands
As we lit the candles, becoming one,
And our life together began.

To have and to hold
Till death us do part.
Vows that we spoke,
They were vows from our heart.

We brought to our marriage our own views
And at times we disagreed.
We talked of our lives, we talked of our dreams,
And each other's side to see.

Our children added to our life.
We watched as they grew,
Guiding them with our hands and heart,
And we prayed for when they choose.

On this day we celebrate
The silver of our years.
We talked of our lives, we talked of our dreams
As we wiped each other's tears.

For we had the calm, we had the storms
Throughout our life,
But our vows stood firm, they never turned
As husband and as wife.

When I was just a little girl
I dreamed of my wedding day.
Color of flowers, gown of white
And of the love I'd give away.

There's one thing that my husband must have
If our life should be,
A love for the Lord, a love so strong,
One deeper than for me.

What's Heaven Like?

When our three children Destini, Damon, and Dustin were teens, they would rather do anything in the world than ask me a question. Because I usually answered them with a question.

At a very early age each child had the same question, "What's heaven like?" Rather than give them an answer, I asked them some questions to help them visualize it in a way that would be meaningful for them. This song came from answers given by our youngest son, Dustin.

My child of six came to me one day he said Mommy, I've got something to say. I've been thinking of this place to see. Will you answer this question for me?

He said, Mommy, what's heaven like?
Can I roller skate, can I ride my bike?
Mommy, are there streets of gold?
Will I see the stories of the people told?
And Mommy, will you be there in case I get
a little scared?

I told my son think of a happy place,
Where he could laugh and with the wind could race.

Where he felt love and safe from the storm, and
they talked of the day when he was born.

Is it like Grandma's macaroni and cheese,
Or when we laugh at Grandpa's great big sneeze?
Is it like when dad wrestles with us,
Or when we ride on his back like a horse or bus?

He said, Mommy, what's heaven like?
Can I roller skate, can I ride my bike?
Mommy, are there streets of gold?
Will I see the stories of the people told?
And Mommy, will you be there in case I get
 a little scared?

I told my son think of a happy place,
where he could laugh and with the wind could race.
Where he felt love and safe from the storm, and
they talked of the day when he was born.

Is it like the weekend campings we go,
Or when we all go out to play in the snow?
Is it like the zoo, the farm, or the park,
Or when you hold my hand when it gets dark?

He said, Mommy, what's heaven like?
Can I roller skate, can I ride my bike?
Mommy, are there streets of gold?

Will I see the stories of the people told?
And mommy will you be there in case I get a little scared?

I told my son think of a happy place, where he could laugh and with the wind could race. Where he felt love and safe from the storm, and they talked of the day when he was born.

With his eyes real big he came running to me
And he yelled, I know what heaven will be!
For the things I love I won't have to roam.
For heaven will be like my home.

He said, "Mommy, I know what heavens like.
I can roller skate, I can ride my bike.
Mommy, there are streets of gold
Will I see the people of the stories told.
And Mommy, I know that you'll be there, in case I get a little scared."

The Pink Tree

She grabbed my hand, my child of three, and yelled,
"Come see what God gave me!"

She pulled me out to the front yard and there for all
to see
Was a beautiful, beautiful, pink tree.

How could I have missed this lovely tree?
This pink tree God gave to my Destini.

My heart did sink as my eyes filled with tears,
As I prayed to God to slow down the years.

To make me forget about the house, chores, and
toys,
And just to play with my daughter and my two
little boys.

To take time to see the world through their
accepting eyes
While jumping in puddles or following a fly.

To tell stories, sing songs, while baking a cake,
Or skip some stones across the lake.

Let the child in me I pray, for I know you will be
there,
helping me find joy in releasing my worries and
cares.

Dear God, I thank you for the gift of this tree,
This beautiful, beautiful, pink tree you gave to my
Destini.

Long Ways to Love Somebody

When our children were little, we got away on the weekends in our pop-up camper. We enjoyed these times with hiking, swimming, campfires, and especially the s'mores. These weekends were the only ones we could afford. But after a long time of saving up, we took a camping trip to Disney World in Florida.

It took two days to get there and two days to return home. There was a lot of stopping, a lot of singing, and a lot of playing games in the car to keep three children happy. All this was done without the assistance of electronics. The only screen in front of us was the clouds during the day, the stars at night, and the Atlas we all used for navigation.

There were so many highlights of that trip, but the one that stayed with me the most was when we returned home. I was tucking our son, Damon into bed and told him I love him. He looked at me and said, "I love you all the way to Florida and back, and that's a long ways to love somebody." His love for me was measured in how long it took to get to and back from Florida, and in his eyes that was a lot. This was the beginning of Damon discovering the immeasurable love of God. A discovery he would appreciate more when he became a parent.

Being a parent is not a popularity contest. While raising our children, we must be parents to them, not their friends. We make decisions that aren't popular and may have to go against the "everyone else is doing it" argument on more than one occasion. It would be so easy to just give in, but we can't.

One thing that I told my children when they were going through those "spreading our wings" years, that I had to answer to God on how I raised them. This was not always well received. Believe me, there were times I didn't want to be the mom, especially with doors slamming, eyes rolling, huffing, puffing, or questionable friends, just to name a few. I read several parenting books, talked with other moms, prayed, slammed doors, rolled my eyes, huffed, puffed, cried, and laughed. More than anything else I wanted them to follow God's teachings. I loved them too much not to make that my number one goal, even if that meant no Mother of the Year award.

Children don't come with instructions or handbooks. However, if we rely on God's love and guidance to help us parent, things are a lot easier - especially when those challenges happen. For God's love, just like Damon's, is a "long ways to love somebody."

Belinda's Hugs

This story is dedicated to Belinda and Matthew, who came into our family when they were six and four and made our family grow in ways we never thought possible.

Belinda was two years old. Every day she put one arm around her mommy and one arm around her daddy and hugged them real tight. Belinda loved to give hugs.

When Belinda was four years old, her mommy was going to have a baby. She was so excited. Finally, baby brother Matthew arrived, and she hugged him all the time. Belinda loved to give hugs.

Belinda had two sets of grandparents. She called her mommy's mom and dad Grandma and Grandpa. She called her daddy's mom and dad Grandma and Poppie. Whenever her grandparents visited, she put one arm around each one of them and hug them real tight. Belinda loved to give hugs.

Belinda thanked God every night for her family and asked him to protect them, especially when she heard her mommy and daddy arguing. She tried to give them hugs hoping that would make the yelling stop, but it did not. When Belinda was six years old, her mommy and daddy got a divorce.

Belinda didn't want her mommy and daddy to get a divorce, and she couldn't understand why God was not answering her prayers to keep her mommy and daddy together. There were so many feelings in her heart. She was angry, hurt, scared, and felt all alone, even when she tried to pray. Belinda loved to give hugs.

When Belinda was six years old, her daddy remarried. Even though this meant her mommy and daddy would never have a chance to get back together, she did like her stepmom - most of the time. Whenever she went over to her daddy's house to visit, she put one arm around her daddy and one arm around her stepmom and hugged them real tight. Belinda loved to give hugs.

Now Belinda had another set of grandparents. She called them Nana and Grandpa. She liked her new grandparents - most of the time. When they visited, Belinda put one arm around Nana and one arm around Grandpa and hugged them real tight. Belinda loved to give hugs.

Belinda's daddy and stepmom were going to have a baby. She was so excited because she was going to be the big sister again. This time the "baby" was going to be twin girls. When the twins were born, she put one arm around Tatum and one arm around Reagan and hugged them real tight. Belinda loved to give hugs.

When Belinda was ten years old her mommy remarried. Belinda liked her step dad - most of the time. Every day she put one arm around her mommy and one arm around her stepdad and hugged them real tight. Belinda loved to give hugs.

Belinda had another set of grandparents. She called them Mamo and Papaw. She put one arm around Mamo and one arm around Papaw and hugged them real tight. Belinda loved to give hugs.

Belinda's mommy and step dad were going to have a baby. Belinda was excited because she was going to be the big sister again. When her baby brother, Jonathan was born she hugged him real tight. Belinda loved to give hugs.

Belinda's mommy and step daddy were going to have another baby. Belinda got to be a big sister one more time. When Jadon was born she hugged him real tight. Belinda loved to give hugs.

Belinda had two homes. Sometimes that was good, but sometimes she was sad to have two homes. When she returned to her mommy's house after visiting her daddy and stepmom, her mommy asked her if she gave hugs to those other people. If Belinda said yes, she saw sadness in her mommy's eyes. She heard her mommy's voice turn a little mean as she reminded her they were not her real family. They were either her step or half family. Belinda wasn't sure if she should hug anymore.

When Belinda went to her daddy's house to visit, he always asked her if she gave hugs to those other people. If Belinda said yes, she saw the sadness in her daddy's eyes. She heard her daddy's voice turn a little mean as he reminded Belinda they were not her real family. They were either her step or half family. Belinda wasn't sure if she should hug anymore.

Belinda no longer loved to give hugs because they made everyone mad or sad, so Belinda just stopped hugging everyone.

Belinda's school was putting on a spring program. The theme of the program was "Animals of the Sea." The teacher told the children they could choose any animal that lived in the sea, and they were to make their own costume of that animal for the program. Belinda didn't even have to think twice about what animal she was going to be. She was going to be an octopus.

Belinda worked hard on her costume. She drew up a design and then gathered all the material she needed. She didn't want anyone to see it until the night of her program.

Her teacher said the class could invite as many people as they wanted. Belinda made up her own invitation and gave them to everyone in her family, the real, the step, the half. And then Belinda prayed.

Belinda was extremely nervous the night of the program. She kept poking her head out the curtain to see if her family was there. She first saw her mommy, step dad, Matthew, Jonathan, and Jaden. Then she saw her daddy, step mom, Tatum, and Reagan. Then she saw her four sets of grandparents. That was seventeen people who came to see her play.

Belinda ran to put her costume on and find her place on stage. The music started and the curtain rose. There was Belinda right in the front with her beautifully handmade octopus with seventeen arms. Everyone in the audience was pointing and talking about her costume. But Belinda kept on singing and dancing.

When the program was over, the teacher explained to the audience that each child was to pick any animal of the sea they wanted to be, and that they were to make their own costume for the program by themselves. The teacher called each child up one at a time to tell why they had picked the animal they had chosen.

When it was Belinda's turn her heart went right to her throat. She didn't think she would be able to speak and that she would start to cry. But she felt God's hand on her shoulder, and the words came. "I picked the octopus because of its many arms. I know the octopus really only has eight arms, but I wanted mine to have seventeen. You see if I had seventeen arms I would have enough arms to hug everyone in my family. I wouldn't have a real family, a step family, or a half family. Everyone would just be my family. I could hug them all at the same time, and then no one would be mad or sad.

It seemed like forever before anyone said anything or even moved. Belinda just knew everyone in the audience was mad at her too. Tears came to her eyes.

Finally, all of Belinda's family stood up. She thought they were all going to leave. But instead, they walked up to the stage and each person held onto an arm, hugging it as hard as they could and smiling. Belinda once again loves to give hugs.

A Song for James

When I became a mother, I couldn't imagine how I could love anyone more than my children. Yet, when those grandchildren came along, I found my heart wanting to burst open with love I didn't know could exist. A love that can never be explained. It did not matter if they came to us by birth or by other means. They were all our grandchildren. This is a song I wrote after receiving a call from our son, Dustin who was at the time stationed in Okinawa.

It's four in the morning and the phone it did ring.
The voice on the end said, "Hello Grandma."
"I'm a Grandma!" I yelled and my heart it did sing
So I woke up your Grandpa who said, "Uhhh, Grandpa who?"

Your name is James Carl, and you are six pounds seven ounces.
Eighteen inches from your head to your toes.
Oh, I can't wait to see you, to hold you, to love you,
Cuddle you tight and kiss your nose.

Though you live far away you will always be near
For I have songs and stories of your family here,
Of your aunts and your uncles, your cousins, and friends.
Your family in the Lord whose strength you can depend.

As a grandma I'm blessed with Belinda and Matthew
and now, little James, I welcome you too.
And when I sit on my porch swing and see the stars in the night,
I'll make a wish for you all and in my heart hold you tight.

Reagan's Ball

We were coming home from church one Sunday night. Our four-year-old twin granddaughters, Tatum and Reagan, were in the car with us. We were about ten minutes from our home when Reagan excitedly yelled "My ball. My ball." Not seeing any ball, I asked her if she left it at church. Tatum turned to her and said, "Sissy, we'll get it next time." Little did they know they would be teaching me a lesson that night.

Reagan was lying in her bed on a sunny Autumn morning, looking at the different colors of leaves on the oak tree outside her window. She noticed that one of the leaves was shaped like her favorite ball. She wanted to play with it, so she jumped out of bed to look for her ball. She looked under her dolls, in her toy box, and behind all her stuffed animals, but she could not find her ball.

Reagan needed help. She woke up her twin sister Tatum to help her. At first Tatum didn't want to get up, but she liked playing with Reagan's ball too, so she got out of bed. They looked under the dog, in the fish tank, and behind the iguana, but they could not find Reagan's ball.

Reagan needed more help. She woke up her older brother and sister, Matthew and Belinda, and asked them if they could help her find her ball. They looked under the couch, in the DVD cabinet, and behind the television, but they could not find Reagan's ball.

Reagan needed even more help. She woke up her mommy and daddy and asked them if they could help her find her ball. They looked under the kitchen table, in the refrigerator, and behind the microwave, but they could not find Reagan's ball.

Reagan had an idea. She called up her Uncle Damon, Aunt Lena, cousins Nikita and Lukas to see if she left her ball at their house. They looked under the computer, in the scanner, and behind the printer, but they could not find Reagan's ball.

Reagan had another idea. She called up her Uncle Dustin, Aunt Maki, and Cousin James to see if she left her ball at their house. They looked under their swings, in the playhouse, and behind the sandbox, but they could not find Reagan's ball.

Reagan was beginning to think she would never find her ball. Then she remembered that she and Tatum were going to Nana and Poppie's house to stay the night. She thought she might have left her ball there, and she just knew Nana and Poppie could find her ball. When they arrived at Nana and Poppie's house, she ran to them and said, "Nana, Poppie, I lost my ball. Did I leave it here?" They looked under the pile of leaves, in the apple tree, and behind the barn, but they could not find Reagan's ball.

They looked in different places all day, but they could not find Reagan's ball, and it was starting to get dark. Nana told Reagan that they would look again tomorrow. Tatum said, "Sissy, when we say our prayers tonight, we can ask God to help us find your ball." "Ok," said Reagan, but Nana could see that Reagan was still a little sad, and she came up with a plan to help Reagan feel a little happier. "Who wants to go outside and sit on the porch swing?" asked Nana. "I do," said Reagan. "I do," said Tatum.

"Will you get your guitar?" asked Reagan. "Will you tell us stories?" asked Tatum. "Sure," said Nana. "I'm coming too," said Poppie.

Reagan, Tatum, and Poppie were dancing while Nana was playing her guitar and singing funny songs. Everyone was having a good time. Reagan almost forgot about her ball. All of a sudden Reagan stopped her dancing, gasped, and yelled, "My ball! My ball! I found my ball!"

"Sissy, you found it! You found it!" yelled Tatum. She and Reagan were holding hands and jumping up and down. They were so excited.

"Nana, Poppie come here," said Reagan. "See my ball?" Nana and Poppie ran over to Reagan, who was pointing to her ball. At first they couldn't find it, but then they followed Reagan's finger. "Oh, what a magnificent ball you have!" said Nana. "I'm so glad you found it. We would have never looked for it there," said Poppie.

It was big, round, white, and so bright that it lit up the whole sky. Reagan, Tatum, Nana, and Poppie tried to jump up and touch it, but it was too far away. Reagan and Tatum stood behind Nana and Poppie and played hide-go-seek from Reagan's ball.

When they finished playing, they all sat on the porch swing and looked up in the sky at Reagan's ball. It was indeed beautiful. Reagan and Tatum were getting a little tired, so they climbed onto Nana's lap, put their arms around her neck, and laid their heads on her shoulders. Reagan's eyes were just about to close when she remembered she needed to do something. She slowly raised her head up, looked into the sky, and whispered, "Thank you, God, for finding my ball. I love you." Then she fell asleep.

The Tatumator

Making up stories and singing was something we did with our grandchildren. What I loved most about those times was that there were no screens in front of us. We only had each other, which I cherish. This was one of our stories.

On Monday, Tatum's mommy was vacuuming the living room. She was trying to move the couch so she could sweep under it, but it was too heavy. Tatum flew into the room and said, "I can move it for you because I am the Tatumator!" Tatum used her pinky finger to move the couch. "Thank you," said her mommy. "You are so welcome," said Tatum, and off she flew.

On Tuesday, Tatum's daddy was working on his truck when a wrench fell under it. No matter how much he tried, he could not reach the wrench. Tatum flew to the truck and said, "I can pick up the truck for you, and then you can get your wrench, because I am the Tatumator!" Tatum picked up the truck with her little toe while her daddy got the wrench. "Thank you," said her daddy. "You are so welcome," said Tatum, and off she flew.

On Wednesday, Tatum's sister Reagan was riding her bike when out of nowhere a big rock wall blocked her way. Tatum flew down to her and said, "I can punch a hole into the rock wall, and then you can ride your bike through it, because I am the Tatumator!" Tatum gave the wall one big hit with her fist and made an opening. "Thank you," said Reagan. "You are so welcome," said Tatum, and off she flew.

On Thursday, Tatum's sister Belinda was out for a walk when it started to rain. She couldn't see anything because it was raining so hard. Tatum flew to her and said, "I can block the rain for you because I am the Tatumator!" Tatum turned her body into a giant umbrella that protected Belinda so she could find her house. "Thank you," said Belinda. "You are so welcome," said Tatum, and off she flew.

On Friday, Tatum's brother Matthew was cutting the grass when for no reason, the lawnmower stopped. No matter how much he tried, he could not start the lawnmower. Tatum flew down to him and said, "I can help you cut the grass because I am the Tatumator!" Tatum got on her hands and told Matthew to hold her legs and push her. As he was pushing her, Tatum started to eat the grass like a lawnmower. "Thank you," said Matthew. "You are so welcome," said Tatum, and off she flew.

On Saturday, cousins Nikita and James were playing in the swimming pool when it started to leak. They swirled around like a whirlpool. Tatum flew to them and said, "I can save you because I am the Tatumator!" Tatum took a big breath, blew hot air into the hole, closing it up, and stopped the leak. Thank you," said cousins Nikita and James. "You are so welcome," said Tatum, and off she flew.

On Sunday, all of Tatum's family was getting ready to leave for church when a big giant blocked the door. "There will be NO church for you today! yelled the giant. What were they to do? Tatum turned to her family and said, "I need a little more help." "I will call on my friend, God." And with that, Tatum told all her family to hold hands and pray for God to remove the giant. They prayed, and God made the giant disappear. "Thank you," said Tatum's family." "Oh, don't thank me." I didn't do anything." "It was my friend, God," said Tatum.

On Monday, Tatum went back to helping others. After all, nothing could stop her because she knew where her strength came from...her very good friend, God.

The Magic of the Treehouse

A story for our grandson, Nikita, who let me play in his treehouse. This is his story.

Nikita loved to play in the treehouse his daddy and Poppie built for him and his brother, Lukas. In his treehouse, he could do all kinds of things, be anything he wanted, and go anywhere he wanted.

One day he was building forts with his legos in his treehouse when he heard someone yelling, "Help! Help!" He said the magic words, "Going up," and he turned into the treehouse.

Now he was ten feet tall and could see who was yelling for help. It was a little girl two blocks away who had fallen off her bike and was in the path of a fast-moving car. Nikita took a big jump, landing right in front of her, picked her up, and placed her on the sidewalk. The little girl said, "Thank you, Mr. Treehouse." Nikita said, "You are welcome. Now you are strong enough to help someone else who is in danger." He went home, where he turned back into Nikita.

Later that day, he was reading a book inside the treehouse when he heard someone yelling, "Stop it!

Stop it!" He said the magic words, "Going up," and he turned into a treehouse.

Now he was twelve feet tall and could see who was yelling. It was a little boy one mile away who was being picked on by some bigger boys. They were pushing him around and calling him names. Nikita took a big jump, landing in front of the little boy to protect him. He turned and told the boys, "Being a bully doesn't make you cool. It only makes you a drool." All the boys ran away with their tongues hanging out and green slime coming out of their mouths and noses. Nikita helped the little boy pick up his toys and fixed some that were broken. The little boy said, "Thank you, Mr. Treehouse." Nikita said, "You are welcome. Now you are strong enough to help someone else who might be teased." He went home, where he turned back into Nikita.

The next day Nikita was playing basketball in the treehouse when he heard someone crying. He said the magic words, "Going up," and he turned into a treehouse.

Now he was fourteen feet tall, and he could see who was crying. It was a little boy two miles away, who was sad because no one would play with him. Nikita took a big jump, landing right in front of him. He asked the little boy, "Would you like to play with me?" "Yes!" said the little boy, and he climbed into the treehouse. The little boy and Nikita played all day long. They were airplanes, boats, and pirates. Nikita told the little boy it was time for him to go home. The little boy said, "Thank you, Mr. Treehouse." Nikita said, "You are welcome. Now you are strong enough to help someone else who is alone." Then he went home, turning back into Nikita.

That night at supper, Nikita was eating his favorite food of macaroni and cheese when Nikita's mommy and daddy asked him about his day. He simply said, "Oh, not much. God and I were playing in my treehouse." His mommy and daddy smiled at each other, for they knew whenever God and Nikita were together, there was magic.

Lukas: The Inventor

Our grandson Lukas loves to invent things using whatever he finds. I am in awe of his imagination, especially when I become part of the invention. This is his story.

It is made from paper, duct tape, paper clips, staples, and anything he found in a junk drawer. To Lukas it wasn't junk, because when he put them together, he made inventions. Inventions that took him anywhere he wanted to go, anything he wanted to do, or anything he wanted to be.

Lukas's mommy gave him a thousand paper towel rolls. He made a race track that went from the basement to the second floor. His daddy gave him a thousand pieces of bubble wrap, and he made a space station that surrounded his whole house. His brother, Nikita, gave him a thousand PVC pipes, and he made the longest slide ever. He climbed to the top and gave himself a big push. He went up, down, and all around. Finally, he landed in Bonfield, Illinois, at his Nana and Poppie's house which is eighty-five miles away.

Nana and Poppie felt a big wind and heard a thud. They looked up, and there was Lukas. They ran over to him, gave him a hug, and said, "How did you get here?" "I made a slide and just slid here." "Well, aren't you clever!" replied Nana. "You must be hungry from your trip." "Yes, said Lukas. Do you have any macaroni and cheese?" "Of course. I always have macaroni and cheese for my grandchildren."

After eating four bowls of macaroni and cheese, Lukas went back to making more inventions. He and Poppie went to the barn to see what there was for him to use. He saw boards, tools, nails, tires, wood glue, just to name a few things. He drew up a plan for an obstacle course. Nana and Poppie watched him build it all afternoon. Lukas stopped once to help Nana make some monkey bread. After all, he needed to keep up his energy.

The obstacle course was literally out of this world. It went all the way to the moon. Lukas, Nana, and Poppie played in it for hours. Climbing, jumping, rolling, swimming, crawling, or running. No one wanted to stop, but it was late. Lukas was hungry and tired. He ate two more bowls of macaroni and cheese along with some cucumbers, took a shower, then went to bed.

Lukas liked to sleep on the air mattress, so Poppie blew it up for him. He ran and jumped onto his bed and laid his head down. Nana went to his bed and told him she too had an invention. "What is it?" asked Lukas. Nana showed him her invention. I call it "The Snuggling Blanket." Lukas smiled, crawled onto Nana's lap, wrapping it around both of them. He soon fell asleep while dreaming about inventions to create tomorrow.

My Grandma

One day in preschool, the kids and I were making up songs. Kaleb asked me to make up one about his grandma. This task was easy since his grandma was my cousin, Myrna. This song came from watching them play and listening to those wonderful stories told by a proud grandma.

Oh my grandma, I love her so.
She makes me happy, don't you know.
My grandma, I love her so,
'Cause she likes to watch me grow.

A magic carpet ride we take.
A chocolate cake we do make.
We pile the leaves with our rakes
And up and down we skate.

With my own brush we paint her walls,
And then we're off to the mall.
She holds my hand, so I don't fall,
'Cause I am still a little small.

She laughs at all the things I say
and I am never in her way.

She says I brighten up her day,
Then we pretend to eat hay.

She saves my papers from preschool.
I fix her TV with my tools.
She lets me go outside when it's cool
And she wipes my nose when it drools.

Oh my grandma, I love her so.
She makes me happy, don't you know.
My grandma, I love her so,
'Cause she likes to watch me grow.

Fingers of her Hands

I was blessed with a wonderful mother-in-law who treated me like her own daughter. Later in life, she was diagnosed with Alzheimer's. When she needed extra care, she stayed between her two daughter's homes and ours. Grandma's job while with us was folding the clothes. Our job was finding them.

She sang at two o'clock in the morning before waking up our children Destini, Damon, or Dustin for school. They told her it wasn't time yet and gently guided her back to bed.

In rare moments she realized what was happening to her. Moments that made her laugh. Moments that made her sad as she tried to hang on to something that looked or sounded familiar. One day I saw her walking around the house touching all the pictures, which prompted this song for her.

She walks through the house and touches her life
with the fingers of her hands.
Picks up a picture and holds it to her heart
To remember if she can. To remember if she can.

In the Spring of her life when all is new
A young bride she becomes.
In the Spring of her life when all is new
She has two daughters and a son.

In the Summer of her life when all is bright
With her children, she does play.
In the Summer of her life when all is bright
She shows them how to pray.

In the Autumn of her life when all is secured
Grandma, she is called.
In the Autumn of her life when all is secured
She watches them grow tall.

In the Winter of her life, there are shades of gray
and her mind grows slow.
In the Winter of her life there are shades of gray
and her memories let go.

The seasons of her life, they were full
From beginning to the end.
The seasons of her life they were full
This mother, this friend.

She walks through the house and touches her life
with the fingers of her hands.
Picks up a picture and holds it to her heart
To remember if she can. To remember if she can.

Eulogy for My Dad

He sings bass to church songs while driving his family to Tennessee.

He sings a song about a drinking duck while pulling a daughter's tooth.

He teaches the teen Sunday school class.

He questions God.

He puts others before himself.

He shows his three daughters the heart of a servant.

He encourages a daughter to go to nursing school.

He makes his daughter's tummy aches go away by simply saying in a high squeaky voice, "Let Dr. Coats look at you."

He encourages a daughter to open her beauty shop.

He is never without a comb in his pocket.

He encourages a daughter to write, tell, and sing her stories.

He has unlimited one-liners.

He teaches each daughter to drive.

He encourages one of his daughters to continue driving after she has several minor accidents.

He disciplines his daughters, who know they have disappointed him.

He is saddened when he must discipline them, but he knows he must.

He gives his grandchildren piggy back rides while wearing a red wig.

He beats the odds of his third back surgery.

He takes his daughters camping in a pop-up camper.

He takes his grandchildren camping in a trailer because they shouldn't be in a pop-up camper.

He slowly walks his first-born daughter down the aisle.

He slowly walks to the casket of his first-born daughter.

He comes home from work to be met at the door by two little girls. They run to sit on his feet, wrap their arms around his legs, as he walks all around the house calling out, "Now, where are those girls?"

He needs help from those two girls to lift him from the bed to the chair, because his legs no longer have the strength to hold him.

He pays his daughters to remove dead mice because the site of a mouse in a trap makes him sick to his stomach.

He gets sick from the medicine he must now take.

He is behind a towel held by his wife, because it never fails that one of his young daughters must use the bathroom when he's taking a bath.

His weak hands try to hold a blanket around himself when his grown daughters help him use the commode.

He drinks coffee from his mug while his great-grandson drinks his "coffee" from a sippy cup.

He uses a sippy cup for his coffee because his hand can no longer hold a mug.

He shows his daughters what it means to be committed to a marriage.

He holds on to this life until he is reassured there is someone to care for his wife of sixty-six years.

He makes funny sounds of belching and passing gas.

He makes frightening sounds as he prepares to leave this earth.

He has a body with cancer that died.

He has a soul with God that lives.

Rooms of December

December 20, 1977. I am in a labor room anxiously awaiting the birth of our third child. I look around and see two generations that will be a part of our child's life.

December 20, 2018. I am in a hospital surgical waiting room anxiously awaiting the outcome of our granddaughter, Tatum's surgery. I look around and see two generations that are part of her life.

December 21, 2018. I am in a hospital room, relieved to hear the words that they got all the cancer. I look around and see two generations that were up all night and anxiously awaiting the words from the doctor, " All is good. You can go home now." I am then reminded of where these generations were the previous December.

December 21, 2017. I am in a room that is filled with family, friends, and hospice. I look around and see three generations that stayed awake for several days, anxiously awaiting the "birth" of our matriarch. She is our mother, grandmother, and great grandmother. She takes her last breath as she hears the words, "All is good. You can go home now."

Section Five - AWWW, or Tissues Optional

Ideas for a story will just hit me by something I saw, read, or heard. Sometimes when I share the idea for a story with a few friends I usually hear the word "Awww," or before I even get started sharing I hear the words, "Do I need a tissue?" Either way, I feel the comments are positive and know these stories needed to be told. The reactions of friends inspired this section.

When to Let Go

A very proud and nervous father sat in the father's waiting room for the birth of his firstborn child. This was the day that he and his wife thought they would never see, for the years before consisted of visits to the doctor and discouraging news. But, today, their prayers were answered.

The father was delighted to hear the words, "You have a daughter," for he wanted a daughter. He was reunited with his wife in the recovery room, and with tears in his eyes he said, "Did you see what God gave us?" She simply smiled and said, "Yes, I was there." As she held onto his hand, he bent over to kiss her and said, "Thank you." He then left with his bag of dimes to call family and friends to tell them of the birth of their daughter.

As their daughter grew, the mother and father experienced the joy and pain of discovering her independence. The terrible twos turned into the terrible threes. There were times of love and times when love was doubted, but giving up was never an option.

In the silence of the night, they prayed:

Dear God, please hold our hands as we hold hers. Help us to guide her, to teach her, to love her, and to be positive, supportive parents. But, most importantly, help us to show her your love so she will want to know you. And, when the time comes, help us to let go of her hand.

As their daughter grew, the mother and father experienced the pain and joy of her teen years. There were times of love and times when love was doubted, but giving up was never an option.

As their daughter grew, the mother and father continued to experience the pain and joy of her of becoming a young adult. There were times of love and times when love was doubted, but giving up was not an option.

A very proud and nervous father of the bride waited for his cue to walk his daughter down the aisle. This was a day they knew would come, and it came with mixed emotions. The minister asked, "Who gives this woman away?" His daughter held onto her father's hands. He fought back the tears as he softly said, "Her mother and I." He kissed his daughter and placed her hand into her husband's and walked away.

In the silence of the night, they prayed:

Dear God, you held our hands as we held hers. You helped us to guide her, to teach her, to love her, and to be positive, supportive parents.

But most importantly, we pray she saw your love and will want to continue to know you, for the time has now come for us to let go of her hand.

Thoughts from a Couch

I am sitting on my couch, in my living room, on what is our third week of below zero temperatures. The frigid Illinois wind chill is making it even colder. All is cozy inside, as I sip my hot tea while viewing the snow out my front windows. I know I shouldn't complain about the weather since it is God's creation. Yet, I do. I know I shouldn't complain as the snow helps prepare the land for planting crops in the Spring. Yet, I do. I know I shouldn't complain while I am warm in my home, while others have only a cardboard box for shelter. Yet, I do.

For the first two weeks of this arctic blast, our home was filled with anywhere from two to fifteen additional family members. There was playin cards and dominos, trying to keep a lighter lit while setting off fireworks, peeking into Christmas stockings, washing and folding clothes, kitchen turned into a stage for magic shows, eating homemade cinnamon rolls, mac and cheese, drinking hot cocoa, hot tea and coffee, a non-stop opening of a refrigerator door, a room filled with air mattress, couches made into beds, and wrestling matches on the floor. I heard laughing. I heard crying. I loved every minute of our gathering.

This gathering came to be because we were brought together to celebrate the life of our mother, grandmother, great-grandmother, and great-great-grandmother. Mom was 91 years old when God took her home December 21, 2017. As sad as her death was for all of us, it was also a time of happiness. I can look back on those brutally cold days having a heart made warmer by the telling of old stories and the making of new precious memories.

I realized while sitting on my couch, that Spring is less than three months away. I wondered if I will complain about the rainy Spring weather. Sadly, I will. When I take the time to find a warming memory it helps me appreciate the seasons God created and my family. However, with the approaching warmer seasons, I may find those memories a little easier from a hammock on the beach.

Jesus is Real

Our granddaughters, Tatum and Reagan, boarded the church bus on Monday, June 25, 2018 to Holland, Michigan for a youth retreat at Hope College. That following Friday they boarded the bus to return to Herscher, Illinois. Excitement filled the bus with talk about the speakers and activities they did that brought them closer to God.

The trip took them well into the early hours of Saturday morning. Somewhere around 1:30 a.m. the children saw smoke and flames. The quick thinking of the bus driver and chaperones guided the children off the bus to safety. Within minutes the bus was totally engulfed in flames.

I can only imagine what everyone was feeling. I can only imagine what the parents were thinking at the moment they received a call from their child. I can only imagine the scene when parents and children were reunited. I can only imagine what everyone was going through when it all sunk in of what happened and what could have happened.

The one thing I don't have to imagine is that I know God was in control that morning.

The children were running from the bus, gathering around to comfort each other, when a billboard

171

was noticed. The sign only had three words. These three words were all they needed to feel God's arms around them. It simply said…"Jesus is Real."

The Old Porch Swing

At some point in my life, I question if I have ever done anything worthwhile. I tend to compare myself with the success of others instead of my own personal value.

Now, being "slightly seasoned," dwelling on these thoughts is not as important. By the end of the day, I am thankful if all my body parts are not hurting at the same time, the car may be held together with duct tape, but it is paid off and I found the keys.

Isn't it too bad we couldn't have the wisdom we obtained from being older when we were younger, to help put our lives into perspective?

As I sat on my porch swing reflecting on my life this song came to be.

In the Summer we'd go to grandma's place,
And from the car I would race.
For there on the front was the old porch swing,
Where I'd dream of my life and songs to sing.
Where I'd dream of my life and songs to sing.

I was a doctor at the age of four,
Owned some horses and a grocery store.
At eight I was a Mouseketeer,
Flew with Superman to calm the fears.

Gonna be a teacher when I was sixteen,
Of the Bible stories and the ABC's.
Eighteen I was gonna save the world,
Make it safe for all the boys and girls.

A happy day in my life.
When I became a blushing wife.
A perfect one I would be,
If only he could be like me.

We had our ups, we had our downs,
We had smiles, we had our frowns.
We found life was not a game,
Where are all my dreams of fame?

Blessed with children even more,
Wanted them to know they could open any door.
Diapers, feeding, and colic too,
Buttons, zippers, and tying shoes.

I turned around and they were teens,
Trying to spread their own wings.

We did laugh, we did fight.
Where are all my dreams of the night?

Now, I have my own porch swing,
And I know I lived my dreams.
A small piece of the world I reach,
In the hearts of the children I teach.

A husband who believes in me,
And that love our children did see.
One day out on my porch swing,
It will hold my grandchildren and their dreams.

In the Summer we'd go to grandma's place,
And from the car I would race.
For there on the front was the old porch swing,
Where I'd dream of my life and songs to sing.
Where I'd dream of my life and songs to sing.

The Bird

In the early Spring of 1985, we purchased something that kinda, almost resembled a house. It was what you call a real handyman special. All the windows were broken, it had three colors of shingles, the living room was decorated by the fuse box and heater. Since there was three feet of snow on the ground, we had no idea what the yard looked like. Yet, we fell in love with the place and could just see its potential. After all, John is a carpenter, and what did we have to lose besides our marriage?

As soon as the closing was signed, sealed, and delivered, we went to work. We shoveled the snow in order to get to the door. Once inside, we started tearing the drywall down. I was in the front room working when I let out a scream. Those who came running to my aid found me on top of the ladder, for there hibernating in the wall was a snake. Since there was no mention of snakes being part of the contract at the closing or within the legal description of the house, I felt it a trespasser, and that a hangin' was in order. Little did I know that snake would be the first of the many critters we would have on the old homestead.

After being reassured there were no more snakes, we continued the remodeling on the back of the house, which would be a bedroom for the boys. As we tore off the last piece of siding, I noticed a nest with the skeleton of three baby birds on the bottom. I thought what might have happened is the mama bird made her nest in the hole we had seen in the top of the siding for added protection for her babies. Sadly, that nest fell behind the siding and got stuck in between the walls of the house and the outside siding.

I instantly felt a bond with that mama bird flying around, hearing the cries of her babies, but not being able to get to them. What an awful feeling for any mother.

We finished the house in late Spring and moved in. Early one morning, the boys were awakened by a beautiful red bird flying into their bedroom window. It flew into the window and back to the tree, into the window and back to the tree, and into the window and back to the tree. At first this was cute, but after the second week of being awakened at 5:00 in the morning, it wasn't cute anymore.

We thought it was seeing its reflection in the window, thinking it was another bird. So John fixed a rod going across the window, but it flew to the window next to it. It flew from the tree to the window over and over again. Then it dawned on us that this might be the mama bird trying desperately to come back to her babies. The room addition now covered the opening to her nest. That didn't stop her. She returned every Spring and continued her ritual of flying to the window and back to the tree.

I didn't realize how much this mama bird and I would have in common until July 11, 1993. We were taking our firstborn, our only daughter, Destini off to school in Pittsburg, Pennsylvania. It was 575 miles from our home, which took about nine hours. After making several trips to unload all of Destini's belongings, we said our goodbyes. As John and I were leaving, tears started streaming down my face. I wanted to run back to her, but I couldn't. I knew I had to leave her. The return trip home took forever. I wanted to get home in case Destini needed to call me.

We arrived home around 9:00 that evening, and I found myself drawn to Destini's room. Then I found myself doing something I said I would never do. I started cleaning her room. I was sorting through her pictures of graduation, prom, and gatherings with her friends. I needed to feel her presence, to hold her, to tell her I love her just one more time. I cleaned and reminisced until about 2:00 that morning and then went to bed.

The next morning I found myself once again drawn to her room. I walked in, wanting something to be messed up, but everything was still in order. Just then, that red bird flew to the north window, and our eyes met for a second. She then flew to the east window. Our eyes again met as those they were inviting me to follow her. Something directed me to go to our backyard. As I walked onto the deck, which was next to the boys' bedroom, I saw her flying to her tree. This time there was something hanging out of her beak. While in the tree, she took great effort to secure the object she had in her beak onto the branch of the tree. When her task was completed, she turned to me, looked into my eyes, then flew away. She never did this before, so I went over to see what she had left in her tree. I stood on my tippy toes and reached for the branch. I looked closer to what she placed in the tree. I recognized what it was. Tears filled my eyes, in my hands I held an apron.

This beautiful mama bird in her own way was telling us both, it was time to cut the apron strings. She never returned.

Are You Better, Bob?

Bob Jewel managed the local Walmart in Bourbonnais, Illinois. When we met him at church we instantly fell in love with his contagious smile.

At an early age Bob was diagnosed with ALS. Even though it took over his body, it never took over his relationship with God or with his family.

I had the blessing of his company one day a week. We shared stories, laughter, tears, movies, scriptures while doing the routine of his physical care. One day several family members came for a visit. Their visit inspired this story.

It was my day to be with Bob. This particular Wednesday Bob's mother, who has dementia, came to visit. While many of her thoughts are unorganized, she has one small, be it ever so slight connection to reality. She knows her son is sick and wants to see him. Her daughter, Cindy, takes the three-hour trip from Peoria, Illinois to bring her to see Bob. I have been to Peoria several times and enjoyed the drive while admiring the scenery, but after spending just ten minutes with Bob's mother, I could only imagine how long the ride was for Cindy, and I admired her for taking this journey.

His mom repeats every sentence three times in a loud voice. But, I couldn't help noticing that every fifth sentence or so is a question asked by a loving, concerned mother.

Are you better, Bob?' "Are you better, Bob?" "Are you better, Bob?

She is unaware of the delicious egg salad that Sandy, Bob's wife, prepared for them, but is proud of the drink she is holding from a stop at the gas station on the trip to see Bob. She proceeds to tell everyone about it several times.

Are you better, Bob?" "Are you better, Bob?" "Are you better, Bob?

There are three generations visiting in the kitchen who are no longer going through the "normal" stages of life. Bob's mother took care of him when he was young, and one day Bob would care for her. But he will not, for he cannot care for himself. Bob helped raise twin sons who are in college. When he is older his sons would be there to take care of him. They will not be taking care of him in his old age. They are taking care of him now.

Are you better, Bob?" "Are you better, Bob?" "Are you better, Bob?

181

Yet, with all the upheaval of the everyday life of this family, they are so normal. They question God but have faith in God. They rejoice in the happy memories and cry for the memories that will not be. They sacrifice their time, and they long for their time. They become angry at all that is happening. They become stronger from all that is happening.

Are you better, Bob?" "Are you better, Bob?" "Are you better, Bob?

Bob's mom walks around the room, leaving for work because it is payday. She walks to a bedroom, trying to find Cindy, as she is convinced it is time to awaken her. She walks over to Bob's bed to show him a picture she made for him in Art Therapy, a class offered in the facility where she lives.

Are you better, Bob? Are you better, Bob? Are you better, Bob?

Bob's mother may not totally understand what has happened. But, if she has that one grasp of reality, be it ever so slight, I pray she knows that yes...

Bob is better now. Bob is better now. Bob is better now.

In memory of Bob Jewel

November 9, 1959 – October 11, 2014

It's Not Just A Table

It is September 8, 2018, around 10:00 p.m. I am sitting on my empty living room floor. In three days, we will be leaving our home of 33 years in Bonfield, Illinois, to move to Ocala, Florida. Even though John and I are excited about the move, it is bittersweet. I can keep it together if I don't have to talk to or see anyone.

What keeps me somewhat sane is seeing how God has orchestrated this move. His plan has been so much better than the one we came up with in January. I can't help but smile and tell people every time I see something He has done for us to make this move as smooth as possible. I am so humbled with all that is going on in this world that He has taken the time to help us every step of the way.

I kept saying I'm not attached to the house or anything in the house. I kept saying I have wonderful memories that I can take with me and add them to the ones we will make in Florida. But, I have to admit, as my kitchen table was going out the door, my heart sank. We purchased it about fifteen years ago from an Amish store. Twelve people could sit around it when using all four leaves. Sometimes we would squeeze in one or more so we could all be around the table.

As they were loading the table into a truck, I could see John sitting proudly at the head of it. I could see four generations sharing a meal at the same time. I could hear the prayers. I could hear the stories. I could hear the laughter. I could hear, "Nana, is there more macaroni and cheese?"

I could see us all cleaning up after the meal, taking out the leaves, to make it smaller so it could be used to play board games or cards. I could hear more laughter, which was usually brought on by Destini, Damon, and Dustin pointing out something I said or did. Not meaning to, I gave them a lot of material.

I know it's just a table, but it was a table that held endless blessings of family and friends. Even sitting on this hard floor, I am still amazed at how God worked in the selling of the table. He made sure it was the last thing sold and who would buy it. It was my friend, Janet. Her excitement to get the table warmed my heart.

I pray she will be blessed with making precious family memories while sitting around the table, and that she always has endless bowls of macaroni and cheese.

Section Six - Reflections

I always had thoughts of writing a book, but kept putting it off for a couple of reasons. One, the few stories I did send in to various publishers were rejected, which was a little discouraging. Second, I realized over the years I had a lot of stories, songs, and poems and really didn't know how to organize them. Ok, there was a third one and that was the question, "Would anyone even want to read my book?" But after taking a few classes on e-publishing and writing skills through our "Master the Possibilities program, I was encouraged to once again pursue my book. I just needed to find the time to reflect on my collection of stories, songs, and poems.

A Moment

In March of 2020, Florida Governor Ron DeSantis announced a stay-at-home order in hopes of stopping the spread of the Covid-19 virus. Leaving the security of our home was limited to essentials such as groceries and doctors. The wearing of masks and gloves was highly recommended and, in some places, a requirement.

John and I weren't affected directly with the loss of jobs, a business, or online schooling. However, we knew those who could not be with family who were dying, sick, in nursing homes, expecting, or their jobs putting them in danger. We had friends who missed the first milestones like graduations, concerts, weddings, or vacations. No one knew how long the stay-at-home would be, but we knew it was far from over.

Yet, in all the chaos, all the uncertainty, John and I found a blessing. The blessing of time. Time we should have never lost. Don't get me wrong, our being together 24/7 was at times a little challenging to see it as a blessing. There were eyes rolling, loud sighs, or going to our own corners for a time out, but a blessing it was.

Each day we shared Bible study and prayer. We read books and we talked. We finished DIY projects in between playing a lot of card games. We discovered more uses for our smart television and phones. We called those with whom we meant to keep in touch. We visited with neighbors in our driveway, keeping 6 ft apart.

On our walks together we admired God's sunrises and sunsets. On one walk we ran into our neighbor Mike Gerbo coming the other way. We stopped to talk while staying on our respective sides of the street. Mike shared with us he was working on a book. A couple of days later he sent me a rough draft of a few chapters to read. These chapters inspired me to rekindle my stories, poems, and songs that I had worked on and off over the past thirty years. Luckily, I remembered the file names and set out to organize them.

Mike's first book, "Pops" soon became available online, which I ordered. Online ordering has become the way for many of us, but even more so as the Covid-19 threat has been growing instead of declining. This also means orders are taking longer to fill. Luckily, I did receive the book without a long wait. While reading his book "Pops" one chapter in particular sparked the memory of a story I had completely forgotten about writing. I wasn't sure of how I saved it, but eventually found its location and added it to my collection.

I now have my stories, songs, poems looking ever so nice on my laptop, but had no idea of how to compile them into a book. Time certainly wasn't an issue since the stay-at-home order was still in effect, but I was going to do it -.whatever it was. I poured a cup of coffee, taking it and my laptop to the table on the lanai. I sat down and my mind went blank. I stopped short of clicking on a game of solitaire when my eyes were directed to the sign on the wall next to me that said, "Give it to God and let it go."

Its meaning became clearer when I reflected on all that had happened the past few months with the nation and my personal life. If there was ever to be a "Moment with Melinda," I first needed to have my moment with God.

Made in the USA
Monee, IL
08 November 2020

46984860R00109